TODAY'S LONDON UNDERGROUND

Front Cover: With a train of 1973 Tube Stock about to rumble past on its non-stop run, D Stock 7061 comes to a stop at Stamford Brook. The line ran through here from 1877 but a station wasn't opened until 1912, with the track layout being redesigned in 1932 to accommodate the Piccadilly Line's extension west of Hammersmith to South Harrow. Oddly, for most of the stations on this stretch there is no platform for eastbound Piccadilly trains to use should they need it, except for the westbound platform. (Saturday 3 October 2015).

Title Page: Thankfully today there is a varied amount of historical items preserved and still in use on the system, and one of them is this 1930's style roundel. The roundel has taken many shapes and forms since it first started to appear on the platforms in 1908 and still does the job for which it was designed to do very well, and adds a touch of class to the system. This vintage example is found at Temple station. (Sunday 26 June 2016).

Back Cover Top: The 1967 Tube Stock design came about from the 1960 Tube Stock prototype trains on the Central Line and the experimental 1938 Tube Stock motor car 10306 which operated in its experimental form entering service on the Bakerloo Line in February 1950, later being transferred to the Northern Line in March 1951, where it stayed until withdrawal in 1978. The stock inherited many of the design features that were modern and futuristic compared to London Transport's earlier designs of rolling stock. Three notable features were the futuristic-looking wraparound cab windows, giving drivers a better view of the track ahead; the two large individual windows on the car sides instead of the traditional four square windows; and doors with windows that curved up into the roof line allowing standing passengers to see what station the train was pulling into without having to strain themselves bending down to check. These trains operated solely on the Victoria Line as eight-car trains with the exception of a few four-car units at a time on the Central Line's Woodford to Hainault branch. They were London Underground's first trains to operate automatically with the driver only needing to open and close doors and push two buttons to start the train. Here at Uxbridge, a train is seen on the stock's 'First and Last' railtour to celebrate its service to the Victoria Line before its withdrawal visiting many places the stock would not have visited before. These trains served the Victoria Line for forty-three years between 1 September 1968 and 30 June 2011. (Sunday 15 May 2011)

Back Cover Bottom: Many enthusiasts will forever have the memory of travelling on the A Stock and especially defying gravity as they were thrown up off the seat cushion as it bounced and rattled at speed over the points at Neasden on its fast non-stop run between Wembley Park and Finchley Road. The tracks and point work are part of the entrance/exit to Neasden depot and sometimes Metropolitan Line trains come to a quick stop here to allow staff to board or alight. Here, A Stock 5124 clatters over the aforementioned points on its way to Baker Street. Some of this stock managed to clock up an amazing fifty-one years of service before the last train ran on Wednesday 26 September 2012. (Thursday 8 October 2009)

TODAY'S LONDON
UNDERGROUND

Reiss O'Neill

PEN & SWORD
TRANSPORT

First published in Great Britain in 2018 by
PEN & SWORD TRANSPORT
An imprint of
Pen & Sword Books Ltd
Yorkshire - Philadelphia

ISBN 978 1 47382 347 1

A CIP catalogue record for this book is available from the British Library

Typeset by Aura Technology and Software Services, India
Printed and bound in India by Replika Press Pvt. Ltd.

Pen & Sword Books Ltd incorporates the Imprints of Aviation, Atlas, Family History, Fiction, Maritime, Military, Discovery, Politics, History, Archaeology, Select, Wharncliffe Local History, Wharncliffe True Crime, Military Classics, Wharncliffe Transport, Leo Cooper, The Praetorian Press, Remember When, Seaforth Publishing and Frontline Publishing.

For a complete list of Pen & Sword titles please contact

PEN & SWORD BOOKS LTD
47 Church Street, Barnsley, South Yorkshire, S70 2AS, England
E-mail: enquiries@pen-and-sword.co.uk
Website: www.pen-and-sword.co.uk

Or
PEN AND SWORD BOOKS
1950 Lawrence Rd, Havertown, PA 19083, USA
E-mail: Uspen-and-sword@casematepublishers.com
Website: www.penandswordbooks.com

Contents

	Acknowledgements	6
	Introduction	7
Chapter 1	Metropolitan Line	17
Chapter 2	Hammersmith & City Line	37
Chapter 3	Circle Line	46
Chapter 4	District Line	56
Chapter 5	Northern Line	84
Chapter 6	Bakerloo Line	104
Chapter 7	Piccadilly Line	119
Chapter 8	Central Line	146
Chapter 9	Waterloo & City Line	165
Chapter 10	Jubilee Line	168
Chapter 11	Victoria Line	183
Chapter 12	Architecture & Structures	202
Chapter 13	Signage & Design	221
Chapter 14	Depots & Installations	243
Chapter 15	Rolling Stock	255
Chapter 16	Engineer's Rolling Stock	268

Acknowledgements

I would like to take this opportunity to give a very big thank you to Brian Hardy for going over the text at such short notice, to check the facts and the text you are a lifesaver and a knowledgeable asset to the enthusiast world! Also, thank you to Matthew Wharmby for his introduction, and Jim Blake, John Scott-Morgan and Janet Brookes for their time, help, and patience.

Introduction

by Matthew Wharmby

London's Underground has undergone considerable change in the last decade alone, for a variety of reasons and with a pace that is both measured and surprisingly speedy when it comes to new rolling stock and changes to its interior; upgrading of stations in time to receive new lines to interchange there; and make existing stations step free for all by installing new lifts. This book takes a look at each line, as well as infrastructure and rolling stock, some of which has or is about to disappear into history forever.

Look and Feel

The introduction in the 1990s of a common livery to replace the cheap but unsightly unpainted aluminium finish on trains has brought some colour and stature back to the London Underground 'brand', disguising the fact that the network is not necessarily in common ownership or under the same kinds of funding and thus leading to a more unified appearance than is the case with London's buses. Internally, carriage refurbishment has been more adventurous, with themed interiors specified to match, where DDA-type regulations permits, the colours of each line. Wheelchair accessibility has had to take precedence over the amount of seating and general standards of comfort, but the trade-off, it is anticipated, will be in air-conditioning and walk-through trains that will operate faster and more frequently due to signalling improvements carried out at the same time.

Stations, Signalling and Infrastructure

Following the completion of standardisation of signs, timetables and publicity on a mixed upper- and lower-case basis, attention has been turned to the long and arduous work of adapting stations and platforms for wheelchair accessibility. This continues slowly where funds are available, work in this respect concentrating on raising platform levels either with humps or throughout. Stations so equipped are differentiated on the Tube map by a wheelchair symbol (filled for train-to-street accessibility or outlined for street-to-platform accessibility, after which wheelchair users are obliged to call ahead for assistance).

Rolling Stock

Much work has been done in the last decade on rolling stock replacement under PPP, new fleets having been introduced to the Victoria, Metropolitan, Hammersmith & City and Circle lines with the District Line D Stock now completely replaced by new S stock.

A mid-life refurbishment is currently being carried out on the rest of the fleet that was introduced in the 1990s to the Northern and Jubilee lines, with the Central and Waterloo & City lines trains receiving theirs in 2012 (Central), and 2011 (Waterloo & City). Looking ahead in the long term, tenders are being invited for a new generation of deep-level trains under the project name Evo. With a lower floor and incorporating weight savings for a higher overall passenger capacity, these would be able to feature air conditioning, an accoutrement demanded for many years by the passenger. It is planned to eventually have all the systems lines operating under Automatic Train operation, allowing higher line running speeds and more trains to run closer together safely providing a more frequent service.

LINE BY LINE

District Line
A complete Rolling Stock replacement has now been completed on the District Line, new S Stock having already taken over completely on the Edgware Road to the Wimbledon branch from C Stock in June 2014. The D Stock on the rest of the line does not (and did not) operate on the Edgware Road to Wimbledon branch due to the cars being longer in length; despite recent refurbishment, which removed the 1980s interior, this stock had departed from service prematurely as the last sub-surface stock designed by London Transport with the final train operating on Friday 21st April 2017, leaving the Bakerloo and Piccadilly lines with the oldest and second-oldest stock respectively. Other than that, improvements are being channelled into signalling, a 24 per cent capacity increase being planned by the end of 2018.

Circle Line
The most significant change to the Circle Line, of course, has been its transformation from a circle to something more akin to a frying pan. Since 13 December 2009, the Hammersmith & City Line's western leg has been tacked on so that the Circle Line begins at Hammersmith and then goes once round the circle to terminate at Edgware Road from the south, after which it reverses to go round in the opposite direction ending back at Hammersmith. That has put an end to the perennial problem with the old Circle in that going round, either wholly clockwise or wholly anticlockwise, with no efficient or logical place to reverse, put undue strain on the track and trains wheels going in that particular direction and would often disrupt the three other lines, the tracks of which it shares. Between 2 September 2013 and 10 February 2014, new S stock trains were phased in, ousting the former C Stock, although the trains survived a few months longer on the District Line.

Hammersmith & City Line
Unveiled in 1990 with its new stand-alone identity after 125 years as part of the Metropolitan Line, the Hammersmith & City Line introduced the pink colour to the Tube map. Structurally, as little has happened since then as one would expect, other than the extension at all hours to Barking since 2009 due to the reversing platform and two middle through platforms at Whitechapel

having been taken out of use to permit Crossrail construction, and to accommodate the building of a bigger island platform to cope with the increase of passengers the new line will bring. The C Stock was replaced between July 2012 and March 2014 by air-conditioned, walk-through S Stock. In concert with continuous signalling improvements, this is forecast to increase passenger capacity on this line and the Circle by 65 per cent by 2019.

East London Line
This short but significant line, until 1988 an offshoot of the Metropolitan Line, and at times throughout its existence operated by the District Line disappears from consideration in this era with its comprehensive reconstruction to form a new leg of the Overground network that brought some colour to the unloved and unkempt North London Line of National Rail. Under these provisions, the line was extended at both ends, the southern end from New Cross Gate first taking over the National Rail tracks to West Croydon and Crystal Palace and would later probe west to Clapham Junction, and the northern end bringing back into use the old tracks that used to take North London Railway services to Broad Street. The former East London Line service to Shoreditch was diverted to the west of that station, closed in 2006, crossing Shoreditch High Street via a new swing bridge and then taking up the Kingsland viaduct that had lain fallow since 1986. From there it turned left to pick up the North London Line as far west as Highbury & Islington. New Class 378 EMUs are in service. While this is an Overground line now by the broadest of considerations, the station frontages have been redesigned in a unique style that bridges both the Underground traditions and modern surface railways. A photo taken on this line can be found in the Metropolitan Line section just prior to closure of the line for upgrade work to be incorporated into the London Overground network.

Northern Line
After a long period with deteriorating rolling stock and given for many years the name 'The Misery Line', the Northern Line was provisioned with new 1995 Tube Stock in the closing years of the last century, replacing rolling stock dating back to 1956, 1959, and 1972 and bringing an end to a long-time tradition on the Underground of trains having guards. Heavy refurbishment was needed throughout the line, however, and multiple closures and replacement by buses was necessitated to accomplish this. The service to Mill Hill East, meanwhile, was reduced to a shuttle service in 2006 at off-peak times. The line's planned extension from Kennington via Nine Elms to the Battersea Power Station site is now in full swing, with perhaps a possibility of a further extension to Clapham Junction. A Night Tube service operates on this line from Friday night to Sunday morning between Kennington, Edgware, and High Barnet on the Charing Cross branch only. An extra order of trains is planned for the Battersea extension currently under construction.

Piccadilly Line
The main change to the Piccadilly Line since the millennium has been at the western end, with the new Heathrow Terminal 5 station and the possible extension to a Terminal 6 should Parliament pass the bill to build the new runway. This opened on

27 March 2008 as a spur, the loop working round Terminals 4 and 1, 2, 3 continuing. The extensive damage to the line at Russell Square caused by the bombing on 7 July 2005 was repaired within a month, services resuming on 4 August. The 1973 Tube Stock has been the mainstay of the Piccadilly Line for forty-four years, this fleet of 87½ trains being refurbished internally by Bombardier between 1995 and 2000 and introducing a themed interior by which the handrails were painted to match the colour of the line. The fleet is nonetheless approaching the end of its service life and will be replaced in the next decade, with rolling stock undoubtedly based on the Evo concept. This line has a Night Tube service at weekends between Cockfosters and Heathrow Terminal 5.

Victoria Line

The first wholesale replacement of rolling stock since the line's introduction in 1968 took place between 21 July 2009 and 30 June 2011, the 1967 Tube Stock in place since new (assisted by some ex-Northern Line 1972 MKI Tube Stock trains converted to match, and inserted into the middle section of the trains formations during the 1990s) giving way to the new 2009 Tube Stock constructed by Bombardier. Comparatively little has needed to be done otherwise, the line having been constructed from new with the then-revolutionary Automatic Train Operation, the precepts of which have since spread to other lines. The original system has been replaced with a like-for-like technological upgrade that has allowed a boost in frequency from twenty-seven to thirty-three trains per hour on this exceptionally busy line. A Night Tube service operates between Walthamstow Central and Brixton.

Central Line

The Central Line's 1992 Tube Stock now finds itself being in service for over twenty years at the time of writing and has had an internal refresh with some cosmetic improvements such as new interior ventilation grilles, seat moquette, and a repaint to the exterior and improved window surrounds has taken place since its introduction. Otherwise plans are few, notions for one proposed line or another (the mooted Chelsea-Hackney Line and then Crossrail 2) to take over services beyond Leytonstone to either Epping or Hainault having died down. The 1992 Tube Stock has about another decade of life in it under current thinking and has been one of the more troublesome stocks with design flaws and a handful of derailments. Night Tube services operate from Ealing Broadway to Loughton and Hainault.

Metropolitan Line

In the decades following the severing of the Hammersmith & City Line and then the East London Line, the Metropolitan Line has settled down, having had a new fleet of S Stock trains to replace the popular A Stock between July 2010 and September 2012. The S Stock of eight-car trains is of walk-through design and has air-conditioning and regenerative brakes. Plans to divert the Watford Branch over the disused Croxley Green branch line to Watford Junction had been given the go ahead, however this has now been put on hold as of December 2017 and whether the extension will go ahead now is not currently known. The line's signalling and electrical supply throughout has been upgraded at the same time to allow a 27 per cent increase in peak-hour capacity.

Bakerloo Line

Celebrating its centenary in 2006 along with the Piccadilly Line, the Bakerloo Line has otherwise lagged behind the rest when it comes to modernisation. The 1972 Tube Stock continues to soldier on in service on the line, though modernisation of the cars took place in the early 1990s and in the last few years a mini-refresh and overhaul was introduced to extend the life of the trains further, no plans exist to replace it until signalling has been upgraded with talk that the final withdrawal of these trains may be as far away as 2026. Similarly, budget constraints have put on hold the likelihood in the near future of the Bakerloo Line resuming its service beyond Harrow & Wealdstone to Watford Junction, as before 1982. For a long time, thoughts have been entertained of extending the line at its other end beyond Elephant & Castle, the latest incarnation of such plans being to construct new tunnels via Camberwell and Peckham to Lewisham and then pick up surface lines to Hayes.

Jubilee Line

In only thirty-eight years since its opening, the Jubilee Line has become the third-busiest on the network. Since the construction and opening of the Jubilee Line Extension in 1999 which replaced the run to Charing Cross, with one through South East London and Docklands crossing beneath the River Thames four times in its journey to Stratford, with much expansion and building developments hastily building up along its route. In the last week of December 2005, the line was closed to admit the introduction of a seventh car to its trains of 1996 Tube Stock, for a 17 per cent increase in capacity and between 2009 and 2010 the signalling was upgraded. Conversion to Automatic Train Operation now permits a frequency of thirty trains per hour and higher line speeds, and this line now operates the weekend Night Tube between Stratford and Stanmore. This line has also been earmarked for an order of some additional trains along with the Northern Line order.

Waterloo & City Line

The self-contained and isolated status of this short but vitally important railway does not lend itself to much activity or variety, but the lifting out of the rolling stock for whatever reason garners much interest. This took place during the wholesale replacement of its Network SouthEast-liveried Class 482s with London Underground 1992 Tube Stock in 1993 and more recently over the summer of 2006, when the whole line was shut down for a comprehensive refurbishment. The carriages were lifted out by crane at the Spur Road end of Waterloo Station near Lower Marsh, leaving room for the track and signalling to be upgraded, which was completed by 2007. Further work is to be done at the Bank Station end by 2021.
This book covers the period from 2007 until the present day.

2013 was a big celebration year for the London Underground as it celebrated its 150th birthday and, just as it had done back in the 100 years celebrations in 1963, there were many and various events throughout the year, both on and off the system. The main event was running Metropolitan Locomotive No.1, restored coach 353 with four Ashbury coaches and a milk van, and Metropolitan electric locomotive No.12 *Sarah Siddons*, which were all former rolling stock of the Metropolitan Railway. The train ran between Moorgate and Edgware Road stations over two weekends. This picture shows the special Underground 150 displayed at the various stations the special train passed through along the original route of the first Underground railway in the world, with photographs of the many staff and developments throughout time. (Sunday 20 January 2013)

London Underground operates two types of rolling stock on its system, both tube stock and surface stock. This example here represents the tube stock variant, which is built to a smaller dimension to fit into the smaller single tube tunnels. This 1972 Tube Stock train on the Bakerloo Line has just detrained its passengers at Harrow & Wealdstone and is going into the turn back siding with 3236 on the rear. The Bakerloo Line used to continue beyond here daily up to Watford Junction until the 1982 service cuts where by that time only four trains southbound in the morning rush and four northbound in the evening rush were operated. This site was also affected by the 1952 British Railways disaster, where a number of lives were sadly lost. (Saturday 4 April 2015)

The Underground can boast many versions of its roundel with many still in everyday use. This 1930s example is located outside Northfields station on the Piccadilly Line's Heathrow branch and is very welcoming when it is illuminated at night time.

The District and Bakerloo lines both share their lines with the successful London Overground services which took over the Euston to Watford Junction Line and the North London Line from Silverlink Metro. Here a service worked by 378 227 over the North London Line section curves towards Kew Gardens having just departed Richmond; this train will share tracks with the District Line as far as Gunnersbury Junction. After the takeover, Transport for London ordered new three carriage Class 378 units to replace the veteran dual voltage Class 313 units which were also three carriage trains, but with such good reliability and frequency as the new London Overground services offered, an increase in passenger numbers saw a fourth carriage and finally a fifth carriage added to their formations. (Thursday 22 December 2016)

Some of London Underground's architecture and history, all in one picture. This small structure found in the centre of Cockfosters ticket hall used to be where tickets were sold to the passengers and many of these types lasted well into the late 1970s in everyday use before the modern style ticket offices, which have since been closed, were introduced. It certainly blends in well with the 1930s art deco train shed, and period signage that has been retained at this listed station. (Saturday 24 December 2016)

Chapter 1

Metropolitan Line

Eastcote is one of the many of Charles Holden's classic art deco stations from the 1930s situated on the Uxbridge branch, with A Stock 5024 at the rear of this departing train to Uxbridge. Charles Holden's design work is often recognisable from the basic drum or box shape surface buildings and platform furniture made out of concrete: however, basic as they are, they still look just as modern and pleasing to look at all these years later, defying the true age of the stations. The Metropolitan Railway reached here when the line was extended from Harrow-on-the-Hill to Uxbridge in 1904, only having one intermediate station at Ruislip, with Eastcote station opening two years later on 26 May 1906. This branch was also served by the District Railway from 1910 but was transferred to the Piccadilly Line in 1933 when it was extended westwards from South Harrow. (Sunday 7 October 2007)

Although it is no longer physically a part of the Metropolitan Line or the Underground network, the East London Line was opened and for many years had been operated by the Metropolitan Line and used its rolling stock. At one time, it ran through services to the line via Aldgate East using a spur off the District Line called St Mary's Curve, just before the District Line enters the open at Whitechapel. At New Cross, A Stock 5113 departs on the rear of this Whitechapel train. Shoreditch was the East London Line's terminus but the line only went as far as Whitechapel in off-peak periods. This picture was taken a few weeks before the line closed as an Underground line for refurbishment to become incorporated into the newly created successful London Overground network. The A Stock was first introduced to the line in 1977 replacing four car 1938 Tube Stock units off the Bakerloo Line and over the years the line has used a very varied range of old and new District and Metropolitan Line rolling stocks. (Saturday 15 December 2007)

At Dollis Hill, under the watchful eye of the rebuilt Wembley Stadium in the background, a Baker Street-bound train of A Stock lead by 5094 rattles past at speed, on its uphill slog as far as Kilburn, with a train of Jubilee Line 1996 Tube Stock and a Chiltern DMU bound for Marylebone in pursuit. Besides the District and Piccadilly lines between Hammersmith and Acton Town running a stopping and non-stop service, the Metropolitan and Jubilee lines here are the only other lines that run in a similar manner between Finchley Road and Wembley Park, although the Metropolitan Line runs stopping and non-stopping trains north of Wembley Park to Amersham/Chesham, Uxbridge and Watford. (Thursday 8 October 2009)

With the rebuilding of nearby Wembley Stadium, Wembley Park station, which was previously rebuilt in 1925 and 1948, had to be rebuilt further with a new entrance to the side also being built, allowing this station to be able to cope better with the huge amounts of passengers who use the station during event times. A Stock 5106 leads a 'Fast Amersham' train into the station, and has offered a faster journey between Finchley Road and here for those who did not want to take the all-stations Jubilee Line. Note that the brick bridge across the tracks seen in the foreground has been retained and shows some design work from the previous architecture, dating from 1948. (Saturday 31 July 2010)

With the upgrade of the Metropolitan Line and the receipt of new rolling stock, London Underground with the new timetable, decided to run through trains all day to and from Chesham off the Mainline, to give passengers from Chesham a train service at similar intervals as Amersham. With the introduction of the new S Stock being one whole train and not two four-car units coupled together as with the A Stock, the Chesham branch could no longer be ran as a four-car shuttle service with new rolling stock. Here we see unit 5090 arriving back at the now disused Chalfont & Latimer bay platform on the last day of the shuttle. It is a shame London Underground could not keep a few four-car units of A Stock and run the Chesham branch as a heritage line, or even use a steam locomotive with some old coaches. The local Mayor also rode on a journey and issued a special ticket to commemorate its withdrawal, and the depot staff did a splendid job at providing a commemorative headboard. (Saturday 11 December 2010)

On a sunny November day, we see new S Stock 21040 glisten in the sun as it draws to a stop at Harrow-on-the-Hill on its run to the City terminus at Aldgate. Delivery of the S Stock was starting to take effect at this stage but the A Stock was thankfully still plentiful. This station is also served by Chiltern Railways trains on an island platform to the far right of this train and Metropolitan trains are able to use all platforms, with the exception of only being able to reverse in platform 2, due to no current rails being in situ south of the platform. This station was given the art deco treatment for its station buildings in the 1930s. (Sunday 13 November 2011)

On a very snowy day at Preston Road, A Stock 5231 leaves for Baker Street with big chunks of snow still on its roof. The staff are also doing a very good job at clearing the snow from the edges of the platforms to make it safe for the passengers to walk and stand waiting for their trains to come. This stock had a tendency to arc quite a lot in wet and snowy weather and often lit up the night sky. This station was opened in 1931-32. (Sunday 5 February 2012)

Amersham is one the Metropolitan Line's four branch termini and is situated in Buckinghamshire. Sitting at 150 metres above sea level making it the highest station on the whole network, it is also the most westerly point of the system, being 27 miles from Central London. In the evening peak, A Stock 5119 waits to depart on the rear of this 'Fast Aldgate' train. This stock was built specifically for the electrification to this point in 1960, the first batch was classified A60 Stock and started to enter service from June 1961 with a second batch being ordered classified as A62 Stock. With the introduction of S Stock and the new timetable, the Metropolitan Line no longer ran fast trains all day in both directions to Amersham; it has been revised to only run fast trains southbound in the morning peak and northbound in the evening peak, probably with much annoyance to a lot of the passengers. (Thursday 5 July 2012)

Many A Stock trains at this point were making the one-way trip from Neasden depot to Northwood via Watford, where a special siding was used to decommission the train, removing parts and releasing all the air from the train. The cars were then separated and loaded onto low loaders to be taken by road for scrapping. Here we see 5094 making such a trip, passing the new order at Pinner, where a new footbridge and lifts were installed at the station in recent years to accommodate step-free access seen in the background. This station was opened in 1885. (Monday 24 September 2012)

Wednesday 26 September 2012 was the day of the last official public run for A Stock with units 5034 & 5063 forming the last train and here we see it departing from the northbound fast platform at Wembley Park, where it came from the depot and entered service during the morning peak. The train visited most of the line's branches this day and throughout the day became swamped by many enthusiasts who came to see the train off. Its last ever public journey was from Aldgate-Watford-Harrow-on-the-Hill, where it detrained and then ran empty to Neasden Depot. Note the last day headboard mounted beneath the driver's cab, a nice touch by the depot staff, celebrating the stocks fifty-one-year existence and excellent hard-working service to Londoners. (Wednesday 26 September 2012)

As with the A Stock a year before, the time of scrapping the C Stock came and followed the same system of scrapping by road from Northwood, where a special siding south of the station was used and altered to allow the train to be decommissioned and separated, then taken away on low loader lorries. Here we see C Stock 5515 leading a train into Northwood before entering the siding on its sad final journey, having just run north to Watford to reverse. (Wednesday 2 January 2013)

Taken from the Jubilee Line platform at West Hampstead, S Stock 21055 speeds past before coming to a stop at Finchley Road. This station was originally opened as a Metropolitan Railway station in 1879, before the tracks were quadrupled from 1938 and all the stations between here and Stanmore was transferred to the Bakerloo Line in 1939. The line was then transferred to the Jubilee in 1979 as part of the new plan to connect the existing section between Stanmore and Baker Street to a new section of line extended towards South East London and the Docklands area. The new line's identity was going to be called the Fleet Line due to its extension passing under Fleet Street towards Docklands but was given the title Jubilee Line as the line was due to be completed and opened in 1977, which coincided with HM Queen Elizabeth II Silver Jubilee; however, the line did not open until 1979. (Tuesday 13 October 2016)

When the Uxbridge branch opened on the 4 June 1904, Ruislip was the only intermediate station between there and Harrow-on-the-Hill. It retains much of its original Metropolitan Railway architecture from the station building to the lovely ornate footbridge near the west end of the platform, which later had a roof put on to protect passengers from the elements. Minor additions are present, such as the 1930s concrete walls for the roundel and posters and modern Health & Safety amenities but thankfully, such architecture and history is still with us to be able to step back in time. An S Stock train enters with 21091 heading an Aldgate train. (Friday 2 December 2016)

Willesden Green still retains platforms for Metropolitan Line trains to serve the station if need be and on occasions when the Jubilee Line had engineering works on the weekend to upgrade the line, Metropolitan Line trains have made stops here to alleviate the loads carried on the replacement buses between Baker Street and Wembley Park. In the above background can be seen the rear of the 1925-designed C.W. Clark station building as S stock 21096 catches up with departing 1996 Tube Stock 96126. With the Jubilee Line upgrade to Automatic Train operation, trains now reach higher speeds between stations cutting journey times and when both trains run together it almost seems as if they are having a race. (Friday 2 December 2016)

The Metropolitan Line no longer serves Kilburn station offering a fast service to Wembley Park. This was site of an incident involving two Metropolitan Line trains when, on 11 December 1984, during heavy fog, a northbound train passed a signal at danger and whilst following the procedure, the driver reset the train's controls and continued to proceed forwards, colliding with a stationary train in front, sadly killing the driver. The 1980s saw the Underground fall into disrepair with lack of money and investment in the system being the biggest danger, as was later seen in 1987 with the King's Cross Fire. Thankfully, in times when more money is being invested into the infrastructure and more precautions taken, such events are extremely rare. An S stock train passes through to Watford with 21060 leading. (Friday 2 December 2016)

Watford is typical Metroland suburbia territory and received its new electric train service on 2 November 1925, opened jointly by the Metropolitan Railway and LNER. The branch is similarly echoed in the Stanmore branch built a few years later in 1932, with C.W. Clark's building designs at street level giving both branches that rural feel. This station is situated some way from the town centre and appeared in the opening sequences of the TV mini-series *Harry's Game* (1982), with a number of shots of the various Underground rolling stock types in use during that period on other lines. This station will soon be a ghost station when the proposed extension to Watford Junction over the Croxley Green branch opens, with a spur near to the Grand Union Canal should this new extension finally go ahead. (Friday 9 December 2016)

All four of the sub-surface lines are interlinked and share each other's tracks as here at Euston Square where the Metropolitan Line shares its tracks with Hammersmith & City and Circle Line trains. This station originally opened as Gower Street, on the original section of the Metropolitan Railway, the first Underground Railway in the world. The station was renamed Euston Square on 1 November 1909 and the widening of Euston Road in 1931, and again in the late 1940s, caused the original entrances to be demolished and reconstructed and today there is no street level building at all. This station retains its 1960s-style continuous name frieze signs just as at Holland Park on the Central Line, and retains large 1960s-style name signs on the walls. Here, S Stock 21084 is on the tail of a departing Amersham train. (Friday 23 December 2016)

Aldgate was opened on the 18 November 1876, on the Metropolitan Railway's extension from Liverpool Street as part of its shared ambition with the Metropolitan District Railway to complete a circular line (now the Circle Line) around the central area of London, linking up all the Mainline termini. The station used to be almost all in the open but in the early 1990s, the northern end of the platform was rafted over to allow development of building above the tracks. The station is also sandwiched between the District and Hammersmith & City Line tracks in a triangular shape, of which both lines' trains can be seen passing very close whilst standing on the platform. The Circle Line also serves here in the outer platforms and one of its trains was to be involved in the 7/7 terrorist bombs, in which sadly many lost their lives. A Metropolitan Line train sits in platform 3 awaiting its departure time, with a vintage platform sign adding a nice touch above left. (Friday 30 December 2016)

On 13 April 1868, the Metropolitan Railway opened a new branch off its original routing at Baker Street where it curves sharply at Baker Street Junction to serve separate platforms, on the first section of the Metropolitan & St Johns Wood Railways branch towards the direction of Willesden. The line serves four platforms at this station, the outer two for terminating trains and the inner two through platforms to and from the City, with the station being reconstructed to this layout around 1925. The line got as far as the distant Buckinghamshire countryside of Aylesbury Town and Verney Junction, with the latter being 50 miles (80km) from Baker Street in 1892, giving it a status as more of a Mainline Railway than Underground. Eventually in 1961, with the electrification of the section between Rickmansworth, Amersham, and Chesham, that is as far into Buckinghamshire that the line reaches from here. A train of S Stock can be seen hiding in one of the bay platforms. (Wednesday 4 January 2017)

Chapter 2

Hammersmith & City Line

The London Tilbury & Southend Railway built station at Upton Park retains much of its buildings and infrastructure, although in the early part of the twenty-first century it received some new panelling on the platform to make the station look a little more modern and to block access to the Mainline platforms that are not in use. The Hammersmith & City Line (part of the Metropolitan Line until 1990) arrived here when it was extended from Whitechapel in 1936, and has seen many periods of operating up to Barking in peak times only to an all-day service. C Stock 5551 gets ready to depart to Hammersmith via Paddington with one of the post-war tower blocks looking down over it in the background. (Thursday 10 November 2011)

At Plaistow in the bay platform 3, S Stock 21325 is about to work its way back to Hammersmith. Plaistow used to be another regular terminating point on the Hammersmith & City Line but in recent years, with the reconstruction work at Whitechapel due to Crossrail and a bid to improve services on the line, it serves Barking frequently all day with this platform only being used for both this line and the District when the service gets severely disrupted. (Friday 10 May 2013)

Hammersmith is the terminus of the Hammersmith & City Line (as well as the Circle Line now) and the line reached here in 1868, retaining much of its original buildings and infrastructure. The line's small depot is also situated here and we see C Stock 5717 departing into the depot, which is immediately to the right of the station and can be seen when departing on a train from any of its three platforms. The C Stock units on the Hammersmith & City Line was getting fewer and fewer by this time; they worked the Circle and the District line Edgware Road to Wimbledon branch a little longer. (Friday 27 December 2013)

With the sun shining down through the roof at Farringdon on preserved Metropolitan electric locomotive No.12 *Sarah Siddons* on the head of a train of old Metropolitan Railway coaches and a steam locomotive, it is running to commemorate 150 years of the Hammersmith & City Line being in existence just as in the previous year which celebrated 150 years of the first Underground railway in the world on the Metropolitan Line. This station has had its original roof replaced and it has been extended to cover the full length of the Underground lines' platforms, the original being slightly shorter. (Sunday 9 August 2014)

Opened on 23 December 1865 as Aldersgate Street, Barbican was a new intermediate station on the Metropolitan Railways eastern extension to Moorgate Street (Moorgate) and would later see trains on the City Widened lines. The City Widened lines were opened and owned by the Metropolitan Railway but Great Northern Railway trains used them between Moorgate and Kings Cross with their services commencing on 1 March 1866. The station saw a name change on 1 November 1910 to 'Aldersgate and Barbican'. The area suffered terribly during the Blitz of 1940/41, with almost all the building being bombed and the station's original roof was to be a victim; of note can be seen the iron supports in the brickwork above which used to support the roof. During the post war years, the lines between here and Moorgate were straightened out and rafted over into a complete tunnel, to allow a new post-war development such as the Barbican Estate and other office blocks to be built to replace the ones lost during the war. The station was renamed as simply 'Barbican' on 1 December 1968. Mainline trains no longer run here. (Friday 30 December 2016)

The Hammersmith & City Line started serving Bow Road from 1936, when the line was extended along the District's tracks between Whitechapel and Barking. Both lines emerge into the open air here as the line climbs a 1 in 28 gradient out of Bow Road, which is the steepest anywhere on the Underground network. Although opened in 1902, this Grade II listed station designed by C.A. Bereton retains a feeling of an early Victorian Railway, with its architecture and its massive steel pillar supports dotted along the western end of the platform. (Wednesday 4 January 2017)

A station once stood on a site near to the current Wood Lane on this line, opened on 13 June 1864 by the Metropolitan Railway under the same name, but would later be closed in 1959. In 2005, work began on the construction of the huge Westfield Shopping Centre, covering a site between Shepherd's Bush and White City, and it was decided to rebuild the Central Line and a new Overground Station at Shepherd's Bush, and at the same time build a brand new station at Wood Lane opening on 12 October 2008, helping to improve the transport links for the area and the shopping centre. The station has a very modern look to it with metal material being used predominantly. Here S Stock 21325 leads a Barking train into the station with continued construction work in evidence in the background. (Friday 6 January 2017)

The curved station at Westbourne Park was opened on 1 February 1866 as 'Westbourne Park & Kensal Green' and was once served by Mainline trains using separate platforms. This station was under British Rail ownership until it was transferred to the London Transport Executive in 1970, but BR suburban trains continued to stop here until trains would cease serving here in 1992, when the platforms were removed and the track layout modified for the new planned Heathrow Express to run. In February 1913, a bomb was discovered here at the station and it is thought that it was planted by a Suffragette fighting for the right to vote; the Underground certainly has been a target both past and present when it comes to letting off bombs! An S Stock train curves out of the station and will descend the underpass passing beneath the Mainline tracks into Paddington. (Friday 6 January 2017)

Chapter 3

Circle Line

A scene you are no longer able to see at Edgware Road is a platform full of C Stock. The C Stock has since been replaced by new S Stock and here we see, from left to right, 5716 on the District Line, 5734 on a terminating Circle Line, and 5542 on a through Circle Line service via Baker Street and King's Cross. The Circle Line shares tracks with three other surface lines and often caused delays and disruption due to it having to be scheduled in between the other lines' trains and having many conflicting junctions with these lines, so in 2007, it was decided to alter the line and extend it along the Hammersmith & City Line to Hammersmith. This helped to boost the services between Hammersmith and Edgware Road and also improved the Metropolitan, Hammersmith & City, and District lines' running. Now the service runs from Hammersmith to Edgware Road, where it completes a full circle via King's Cross and Liverpool Street back to Edgware Road where it terminates. Then, in the opposite direction, it completes a full circle back to Edgware Road via Victoria and Embankment, continuing on to Hammersmith. This has improved the reliability and frequency of all lines concerned. (Tuesday 10 January 2013)

Hammersmith has been the terminus of the Circle Line since December 2007 and now shares tracks with the Hammersmith & City Line. C Stock 5602 slowly pulls in to a stop, as 5542 waits to depart at the tail of a Hammersmith & City Line service to Barking. These trains entered service in two batches; the first were classified C69 Stock, with the first entering service in 1970 for the Hammersmith and City (Metropolitan) and Circle lines, comprising thirty-five six-car trains plus a spare two-car unit. They replaced the CO/CP Stock allowing it to transfer to the District Line to replace the older Q Stock, with a further order placed for another eleven six-car trains to start replacing CO/CP Stock on the District Line Edgware Road to Wimbledon branch, these first entering service in 1978. Both batches were easily identifiable C69s, having black painted roofs and the C77s white; both batches were intermixed, causing trains to run in service with an array of multi-coloured roofs. But after refurbishment, the use of corporate livery made both batches unidentifiable except from their car numbers. (Tuesday 27 August 2013)

High Street Kensington has four platforms; two are terminating platforms to the left of the trains used by the District Line's Olympia shuttle and the two through platforms seen here are used by the District and Circle lines to and from Edgware Road. Here we see S Stock 21538 departing on the Circle Line to Edgware Road and 21343 coming to a stop on a District Line service to Wimbledon. The C Stock which once operated these two services are now history and these S Stock trains form part of a standardised fleet on the whole sub-surface network, offering air conditioning and a walk-through saloon so passengers can walk through the entire length of the train freely and offering more standing space. They are also made up of longer cars, these being seven-car length, replacing a six-car C Stock train, meaning that sometimes more than one set of doors need to be isolated at station stops. (Monday 3 August 2016)

Notting Hill Gate station was opened by the Metropolitan Railway on 1 October 1868 as part of its extension from Paddington to Gloucester Road in its ambition to operate a circular railway around London, connecting up with all the Mainline termini stations which all stopped short of the central area due to concerns that London was cramped enough with slums and small, closely packed streets. The District was also to help operate the service. The Central London Railway (Central Line) reached here on 30 July 1900 and both lines had separate station buildings, but nowadays there are direct connections between all lines and it is now the District and Circle lines that share these platforms. This station is one of the now few to retain its original train shed roof and brickwork from when the line opened and the original gas light fixtures have been retained as the stations lighting, albeit no longer using gas. (Friday 4 November 2016)

Ladbroke Grove serves a very vibrant community and is host to the famous Portobello Road Market and the annual Notting Hill Carnival, which passes beneath the railway bridge and in front of the station. The Metropolitan Railway was extended through here from Paddington to Hammersmith on 13 June 1864 and at the time was an area full of overcrowded and run down slum houses which lasted until the 1970s, when they started to be cleared in order for the Westway motorway to be built through the middle. S Stock 21530 is stopping on a Circle Line train to Edgware Road via Paddington and Liverpool Street. (Wednesday 26 October 2016)

Opened on 30 May 1870, Blackfriars was the terminus of the District Railway before its 1871 extension to Mansion House and its 1884 extension from Mansion House to Tower Hill (named Mark Lane from 1884-1946), where it connected up to the other end of the Circle Line completing the circle. The station interchanges with the Mainline train station built above by the London, Chatham, & Dover Railway opened in 1886, which today is served by South Eastern trains and Thameslink services running between Bedford and Brighton. As part of the Thameslink programme, this station closed between 2009 and 2012 to have its station building and platform layout rebuilt. The office building built above the old station was completely demolished and rebuilt to a more modern design and a new shared ticket hall was built with escalators and lifts between mezzanine level for the Mainline services and below for the Underground services. At platform level, new tiles and coverings were used on the walls and columns as seen here with this 'Outer Rail' Circle Line train pulling in with 21434 leading. (Friday 2 December 2016)

It is not hard to imagine the early steam trains running through platforms 5 & 6 at Baker Street, with the steamy atmosphere and smell of the steam and sulphur. These two platforms sit on the original routing between Farringdon and Bishops Road (Paddington Hammersmith & City/Circle Line station) and they were restored in the 1980s to as nearly original condition as possible and invoke the Victorian atmosphere with the limited lighting. The Metropolitan Line curves off sharply to the right just before the station and serves its own four platforms. This station has the most platforms at any one station on the network boasting ten, four for the Metropolitan Line, two for the Hammersmith & City/Circle lines, two for the Bakerloo Line, and two for the Jubilee Line. (Sunday 1 January 2017)

Cannon Street opened to passengers on 6 October 1884 as part of the joint extension with the Metropolitan District and Metropolitan Railways to complete the Circle Line and an extension down to New Cross on the East London Railway. The station was reconstructed between 1968 and 1975 and in recent times saw further reconstruction to its station building and ticket hall area, which is incorporated into the Mainline station building and new office block above. The station is mainly used by the many office workers in the maze of office blocks surrounding the station and is a shorter walking distance at street level to Bank station than Monument. A D Stock train departs in the distance leaving a Circle Line train in the platform. (Wednesday 4 January 2017)

Opened on 24 December 1868 by the Metropolitan District Railway, the station at St James's Park originally allowed daylight down onto its platforms, but would later be rafted over to allow an office block to be constructed above it. A building was constructed above its eastern entrance and was to be London Transports Headquarters called '55 Broadway' with its clean modern lines and architecture and for many years was the tallest building in London, which by today's building heights in London seems rather tiny. As a train of S Stock enters the eastbound platform we can glimpse the tiles that have remained unchanged since the platforms received them during its 1920s modernisation; examples of the same tiling can be found on the southern section of the Northern Line to Morden. (Saturday 7 January 2017)

Chapter 4

District Line

Richmond sees D Stock 7040 awaiting its lengthy run back to Upminster; time was running out for this stock in un-refurbished condition, as the majority of the fleet had been refurbished. The last un-refurbished train ran on Friday 15 February 2008 comprised of units 7534 on the western end and 7115 on the eastern end. The District started serving here in 1877, using tracks opened by the London & South Western Railway which ran to Ravenscourt Park running on separate tracks to the District on what is now the eastbound District and Piccadilly Line tracks between Turnham Green and Ravenscourt Park. It then travelled on a viaduct connecting to the Metropolitan Railway at Hammersmith, of which the remains can still be seen when travelling on trains between Ravenscourt Park and Hammersmith (District/Piccadilly Line) station. (Tuesday 13 November 2007)

Between Acton Town and Barons Court, the District and Piccadilly lines run side by side, with the District serving all stations and the Piccadilly running non-stop between Acton Town and Hammersmith, with exception of serving Turnham Green on early morning and late evenings and the odd occasion during disruption and engineering works on the District Line. Here at Chiswick Park, D Stock 7060 motors out of the station after the Piccadilly Line 1973 Tube Stock train that has just passed through at speed. (Thursday 21 February 2008)

On a very snowy day which brought London almost to a complete standstill, D Stock 7060 cautiously comes to a stop at Dagenham East on a Wimbledon train. The snow brought a lot of operational problems and disruption for the Underground and further pressure was added by all of London's buses being suspended well into the evening peak. Dagenham East was the site of a very tragic accident on 30 January 1958, when around 19:34 in a thick blanket of fog, a late-running Mainline train collided into its leader that was also running late, due to one of the trains passing a signal at danger. Sadly, ten passengers and four railwaymen were killed. The heavy London fogs and the rundown state of British Railways' infrastructure and trains due to the Second World War probably did not help matters in preventing such tragedies and the station is apparently haunted by a lady with a head injury, who is said to have been one of the passengers who lost her life in the crash. (Monday 2 February 2009)

Upminster is the line's eastern terminus and site of the line's other depot; D Stock 7109 is at the tail of another Wimbledon train as it departs with the snow starting to fall again. Note the large amounts of snow still present on the roof of the train which on occasions could give an unsuspecting passenger a shock when it falls off. This must have been a stressful morning rush hour journey for many commuters, but thankfully all drivers and staff concerned tried their best to keep London moving. (Monday 2 February 2009)

On a beautiful summer's day, D Stock 7045 pulls into East Ham with a train for Upminster, as the morning summer sun shines down. On the eastbound platform, there is an old bay platform where British Railways trains used to terminate on the Kentish Town and St Pancras shuttle service. The District Line's Little Ilford depot was situated just east of the station but was replaced in 1958 after Upminster depot was built; the depot was demolished and a new depot was built for British Railways' London, Midland, & Scottish Railway line and continues to be a depot for its predecessor's trains in the privatisation era today. (Saturday 5 June 2010)

At Ealing Broadway, D Stock 7123 takes a rest before its departure at the head of a service only going as far as Hammersmith due to engineering works. In the background can be seen the roof covering the end of the platform and footbridge over the tracks and looks of very traditional Victorian design. I wonder how many passengers today realise that District trains once continued to Windsor over the Great Western Railways tracks between 1883 and 1885, the District also operating joint services with the London, Midland, & Scottish Railway between Ealing Broadway, Southend, and Shoeburyness between 1910/11 to 1939 just after the outbreak of the Second World War. (Sunday 15 May 2011)

The Olympia shuttle is usually the preserve of D Stock but due to engineering works, trains of C Stock were being used instead, as seen by 5725 at the head of this train which is only going one stop to Earl's Court, where it will reverse from east to west from platform 2 to platform 3 via the crossover east of the station. London Overground on the Stratford and Clapham Junction Line serves here as does the less frequent service operated by Southern. The station has changed greatly since opening in 1864, with the Metropolitan Line operating a service through here from Earl's Court, connecting to the Hammersmith branch just before Latimer Road station with services ceasing in 1940 during war time and never reinstated. The London & North Western Railway also ran a service between Earls Court and Willesden in the early years of electrification. (Sunday 7 August 2011)

At Upton Park, the original home of West Ham United football club, D Stock 7094 stops, bound for Ealing Broadway. These thirty-seven-year-old trains once comprised 75 six-car trains; and numbered nine trains for service as of January 2017 as the S Stock replaces them, but nonetheless still look a sleek and modern design thirty-seven years after replacing the elegant flare sided CO/CP and R Stocks between 1980 and 1983. They are unique as, being surface stock, they are fitted with the same tube sized wheels as the 1973 Tube Stock on the Piccadilly Line, being the only example of Mainline sized stock having tube sized wheels. (Thursday 10 November 2011)

District trains arrived through West Ham in 1902, a year after the London, Tilbury & Southend and North London Railways opened the station; it was not until 1999, when the whole station was rebuilt, that Southend trains gained an island platform again, in connection with the new Jubilee Line extension to Stratford. The Docklands Light Railway has since taken over the North London Line tracks through here and now operates between Stratford International and Woolwich Arsenal, opening in 2011. West Ham was the scene of an IRA bomb attack on 15 March 1976; a Metropolitan (Hammersmith & City) Line train was departing towards Hammersmith when the bomber took a wrong train and changed to go back towards the City. However, the bomb detonated and a passenger tried to stop him escaping but was shot and injured. He then proceeded to run through the driver's cab and escape onto the tracks; sadly, the driver was shot dead trying to apprehend him. Here, D Stock 7072 leads this Ealing Broadway bound train into the platform having just passed over the recently installed turn-back siding, replacing the one at Whitechapel. (Thursday 18 October 2012)

2012 was an important year in the Underground systems history as for the time in its existence, it would play a crucial role in transporting spectators to the London Olympics venues just as it had done back in 1948. D Stock driving motor car 7007 took part in the torch carrying relay in the morning rush hour on Tuesday 24 July 2012 between Wimbledon and Wimbledon Park stations on the District Line, with the front end of the car having the Olympic rings added for the occasion. This picture was taken when the Olympic logos were soon to disappear from this motor car as the train awaits departure from Upminster, on its long run west to Ealing Broadway. (Saturday 10 November 2012)

With the now-demolished Earl's Court exhibition centre looking down over West Brompton station, a now-withdrawn C Stock train motors out for Edgware Road with 5733 on the rear. These trains served the Edgware Road to Wimbledon branch from 1978, when a further eleven trains were ordered to supplement the original thirty-five trains that entered service from 1970, helping to replace the much loved CO/CP Stock. This station is also an interchange with the London Overground's Stratford to Clapham Junction Line. The line reached here in 1869 and it was the terminus of the branch until a further extension was made in 1880 as far as Putney Bridge. This was the penultimate and last full day of service of the C Stock, with the final train being withdrawn early the next day just before the end of the morning peak. (Wednesday 2 July 2014)

Turnham Green sees the new order as S Stock 21402 departs at the rear of this Richmond train. This station is where the Ealing Broadway and Richmond branches diverge and is served by Piccadilly Line trains in the early mornings and late evenings. Having climbed out of Hammersmith, the lines run along viaduct and at an elevated level to just before Acton Town. (Sunday 26 June 2016)

In June 2016, the bay platform at Putney Bridge was converted into a new through platform making the outer platform disused. This was the terminus of the branch from 1880 to 1889, before being extended across the River Thames to Wimbledon. S Stock 21532 departs for Edgware Road, whilst the newly installed clean ballast and track work can be seen on the new westbound platform. (Sunday 26 June 2016)

As part of the tube upgrade programme, many stations are being modernised and as seen here, Sloane Square has lost its distinctive green tiles for these new modern white and blue ones. It has retained its vintage clock, however, seen here as S stock 21433 pulls into a stop on its way to Barking at twenty-three minutes to twelve, with the next stop at Victoria also receiving upgrade work at the time of writing. This station received an upgrade in 1940 and had brand new escalators installed but was to become the site of one of the Underground's worst wartime tragedies during the Blitz when, one evening at 10pm, the station suffered a direct hit causing a huge lump of concrete to fall through the station roof and onto the rear car of a crowded train that was departing the station. This caused seventy-nine casualties, destroying the station and its newly installed escalators in the process. (Saturday 2 July 2016)

Old and new meet at Ealing Common, as new S Stock 21355 on its way to Upminster pulls into the 1930s rebuilt station which still looks as clean and modern as it did when new. Many of these stations have stood the test of time and have thankfully been given Grade II listed status. The line's other depot was opened here in 1905 and has seen some modernisation work at the eastern end to accommodate the new S Stock, which can be seen whilst travelling on the train between here and Acton Town. (Wednesday 3 August 2016)

Earl's Court is the hub of the District Line, with all its branches converging and branching off here. S Stock 21337 waits for the green signal from platform 2 to cross-over onto the track from platform 1 to Edgware Road, having just came off the Wimbledon branch. A new crossover has since been installed allowing trains for Edgware Road coming off the Wimbledon branch to cross over into platform 1 as well as platform 2, which would be more convenient and flexible for the service, with some trains having to be held outside the station and give way to other trains. This station was originally sited a little further east when it opened in 1871. Having suffered a fire in 1875, it was later re-sited to its current position in 1878. This station is also a crew change-over point for drivers. (Wednesday 3 August 2016)

West Kensington station was opened in 1874 and retains many of its original buildings and structures like the platform canopies as we see S Stock 21391 coming to a stop on its way to Tower Hill. This station was originally called North End Fulham when opened but was renamed to West Kensington in 1877. It is the site of London Underground's training centre at nearby Ashfield House. Trains can also access nearby Lillie Bridge depot just to the east of the station and it has been converted from an engineer's train depot to a service train depot in recent times as part of the District Line upgrade with new S Stock. (Wednesday 3 August 2016)

S Stock 21412 is on the tail of a train heading eastbound from Richmond and has just left the shared line with London Overground's North London Line at Gunnersbury Junction. It is passing under the District and Piccadilly lines to join the branch from Ealing Broadway. Although the Richmond branch does not serve Chiswick Park, it passes close by, with the station being to the left of the train. The line was extended to Richmond over the London & South Western Railway's tracks in 1877. (Tuesday 27 September 2016)

Wimbledon Park was reached in 1889 and retains its original London & South Western Railway platform and station buildings at street level as can be seen in the background as S Stock 21410 departs for Edgware Road. Trains departing to Wimbledon pass the nearby National Rail depot of the same name and there is a connection to the Mainline tracks that certain Mainline trains use to travel to and from East Putney reconnecting to its Mainline tracks, so that it can retain running rights over this stretch of line. (Thursday 13 October 2016)

Bromley-by-Bow was originally named Bromley and was renamed in 1967. The station was served by Mainline trains with a connection to the London & Blackwall Railway, now a section of the Docklands Light Railway branch to Stratford from Poplar, which the District Line passes over before curving round to descend into Bow Road. Much development work has taken place around the station in recent years and the apartments on the right stand on the site of what used to be St Andrew's Hospital, opened in 1871 as an asylum. (Friday 14 October 2016)

Becontree was the name of the new housing estate being built between 1921 and 1934 by the London County Council to try and move people out of the East End slums and improve social living conditions; it covers a large area of the nearby land known as the Becontree Estate. During its construction, it had its own temporary railway system that ran from the Great Eastern Mainline at its Goodmayes goods yard running east to near Chadwell Heath where it turned southwards through the future estate towards the Thames, where a 500ft jetty allowed boats to deliver materials and take away the spoil. It used standard gauge locomotives and the line was just over three miles long. It remains the largest public housing development in the world, occupying 3,000 acres of what was farmland and market gardens. In more modern times, we see S Stock 21462 arriving with a train to Richmond. It just shows how populated the area is; as if you were to travel in the morning peak from Upminster towards Central London, the train is already busy by the time it arrives at Barking. (Friday 14 October 2016)

A number of stations east of Bromley-by-Bow owe their origins to the London, Tilbury & Southend Railway, with much of their station buildings at both street and platform level showing its design influence. Hornchurch was re-opened in 1932 as part of the District Line's Upminster extension and at the time the Mainline was under ownership of the London Midland & Scottish Railway of which its architecture influence can been seen in the new style of station canopy from the traditional wooden style. (Friday 14 October 2016)

Stepney Green was opened on 23 June 1902 as part of the line's extension east to Barking, which opened a few weeks earlier on 2 June. The platforms were built to a basic design and the brickwork was painted white sometime later, giving it rather a bit of a clinical look. The Hammersmith & City Line also shares this station up to Barking. (Friday 11 November 2016)

Mansion House originally boasted two island platforms with three sets of tracks, and had a small workshop where the District Railway maintained some of its steam locomotives. It has been largely reconstructed over time and today has only three platforms and had a bay platform like at Tower Hill; this was decommissioned in 2016 and the track has since been removed. The station used to let daylight in through its roof but today the station is completely underground due to a development being built above necessitating its closure between 29 October 1989 and 10 February 1991. Here, a train of D Stock is closing its doors departing for Richmond with double ended unit cars 17534 and 7534 in view. (Wednesday 21 December 2016)

Temple was for many years a station that was closed on Sundays with trains running through non-stop, however, the increase of weekend patronage on the Underground in recent decades has seen all stations except for the Waterloo & City Line opened daily. This station has received new tiling, replacing a greenish colour scheme and also receiving the new style of roundel signs, seen here attached on the wall. A Tower Hill bound S Stock tailed by 21550 can be seen departing with a trickle of light shining down from a gap in the roof, which would have been used to allow the steam to be expelled from the steam locomotives before electric traction arrived. (Friday 23 December 2016)

Monument marks the location of the starting of the Great Fire of London that gutted the area inside the old Roman city wall. The fire raged from Sunday 2 September to Wednesday 5 September 1666, consuming 13,200 houses, 87 parish churches, the original larger timber built St Paul's Cathedral, but miraculously only killing six people. A concrete monument was erected to mark the location of where the King's Bakers stood where the fire began, hence the station's name. It opened on the 6 October 1884 as Eastcheap, but was renamed a month later as The Monument on 1 November 1884, later losing the 'The'. Monument has had a connection to Bank station since 18 September 1933, allowing passengers to interchange trains between the two below ground, but depending on what line you are changing to it can sometimes be quicker to do the walk above ground compared to the long passageways and up and down the many escalators and stairs. Here, a train of new S Stock curves in on a Wimbledon train as a veteran train of D Stock pauses on its way to Upminster with 7070 and 17070 nearest in view. (Saturday 24 December 2016)

The station at Aldgate East was a new station opened on the 31 October 1938, replacing an earlier one that was sited slightly west of today's station. The original station sat very close to Aldgate station and as part of the London Passenger Transport Boards 1935-40 New Works programme, enlargement work to the triangular junction at Aldgate was carried out to allow a more subtle curve to the track work and to make sure that District trains could be held at signals without fouling the points and signals elsewhere. This station sits in a very famous area that was often the place where new immigrants would come and settle and is best known for nearby Brick Lane, Petticoat Lane Market, and the famous serial killer Jack the Ripper who mutilated his victims in the nearby alleyways during the summer and autumn of 1888 causing much fear in Victorian London. (Friday 30 December 2016)

Chapter 5

Northern Line

At East Finchley, the line climbs to the surface where the station has a four platform layout that was rebuilt and opened for the Northern Line on 3 July 1939. This station used to be part of the London North Eastern Railway (LNER) line from Kings Cross to Edgware, High Barnet, and Alexandra Palace and it was intended by the London Passenger Transport Board to take over the line and join it up to the Northern City Line to Moorgate at Finsbury Park. Much of the infrastructure work was carried out and a new depot for the line built at Aldenham, which later became London Transport's Bus Overhaul Works but the Second World War and much politics prevented the project from continuing during the post war years. We see 1995 Tube Stock 51526 and 51531 both terminating in the middle platforms coming from the north due to a severe service disruption; the only time trains usually use these middle tracks is to gain access to and from the sidings at Highgate, which is situated a little south of the station. A northbound service can also be seen departing in the platform opposite. (Tuesday 10 January 2013)

The LT Museum has brought their preserved four-car unit of 1938 Tube Stock out onto the Northern Line, with its red paintwork glistening in the hot summer's sun. Here we see it in the hands of very experienced Motorman Wright climbing the grade up into Brent Cross Station where it would have seen the 1938 Tube Stock work for many years until 1978, with a brief return between 1986 and 1988, the stock just about making it into fifty years of service. The 1938 Tube Stock first entered service on the Northern Line on 30 June 1938, the Bakerloo Line on 2 January 1939, and the Piccadilly Line some years later on 12 November 1951 with this particular unit 10012 along with sister unit 11012 operating on all three lines throughout its career. This stock is one of the many classic stocks designed by London Transport and thankfully a handful of two-car units still soldier on in service on the Isle of Wight at the time of writing, seventy-nine years after they were built, but for how much longer is not known. This station originally opened as 'Brent' in 1923 as part of the Edgware extension and was later renamed 'Brent Cross' in 1976 when the nearby shopping centre of the same name was opened. (Sunday 21 July 2013)

At Colindale station, we see 1995 Tube Stock 51664 heading a Morden via Bank service into the station with quite a few people waiting to board. To the right of the train can be seen space which looks as if it should accommodate another track, to provide an overtaking line for express trains to Central London and the City in the 1920s, but the plan was abandoned. These spaces are common at some stations on the Edgware branch and can be noticed at Brent Cross also. Colindale also serves the nearby RAF Museum. (Saturday 30 November 2013)

Archway was once the terminus of the Charing Cross, Euston, & Hampstead Railway, opened in 1907 as Highgate, it still has a turn back siding for trains to reverse here. It was then renamed Archway (Highgate) in 1939, before its final renaming to Archway in 1947. The big road junction above at the time of writing is in the middle of being redesigned to make it safer for pedestrians, cyclists, and flow of traffic as well as improve how the area looks cosmetically with many new buildings also being developed. (Monday 16 November 2015)

The line was extended northwards as far as East Finchley from Archway in 1939 with Highgate being the next intermediate station, however, it was not opened until two years later, in 1941. Highgate station is an unusual station in that it was built to accommodate nine-car trains, when London Transport trialled them to try to combat overcrowding problems. Here, we see 1995 Tube Stock 51563 at the rear of a High Barnet service making a stop. This station is a well patronised station and would have been an even busier interchange station had London Transport been able to continue with the Northern Heights extensions. This station for many years was known as Highgate low level station, in that the extension would have served a station above ground known as the Highgate High Level; the stations were not officially named this on its signs and the map. (Monday 16 November 2015)

Interchange is provided with the Piccadilly Line at Leicester Square and is a busy station due to all the local cinemas, theatres, and clubs being located around the station. At platform level, both lines received tiling with a theme to the local cinemas, in the form of film camera rolls as can be seen on the top and bottom of the wall in view. The Piccadilly Line served here first on 15 December 1906, with the Northern Line a year later on 22 June 1907. The station has three station buildings at street level from varying time periods and provide much needed entrances/exits to aid the huge traffic flows. Covent Garden on the Piccadilly Line is approximately a five minute walk and is the shortest distance between stations on the Underground at just 0.16 miles. (Monday 23 May 2016)

Kennington has four platforms today, two for the Bank branch opened in 1890 by the City & South London Railway and two for the Charing Cross branch opened in 1926 by the London Electrics Railway, with a loop line for the Charing Cross branch which opened in 1926 at the same time the Morden extension was opened. A junction was made between the two branches during the Morden extension, so that South Londoners were able to have a choice of two routes into the centre of London. This station is unique as it is possible today to depart on a train from the southbound Charing Cross branch platform here and then reappear on the northbound platform a couple of minutes later via the loop, which this train of 1995 Tube Stock is about to do with 51712 on the rear with its destination display already changed for its northbound journey to High Barnet. (Friday 11 November 2016)

The Northern Line now incorporates part of what was the first deep level electric tube railway in the world opening between King William Street (near Bank) and Stockwell at about 3½ miles in length, by the City & South London Railway opened by the Prince of Wales (later to become King Edward VII) on 4 November 1890, public services commencing a month later on Thursday 18 December. The tunnels were built to a much smaller dimension than today's standards at 10ft 6in so when in the 1920s the line was extended further southwards, it was decided to reconstruct the tunnels and stations on the original section to the dimensions of the standard size used on other tube lines in existence at that time. Some of the stations on the southern section were rebuilt to the larger dimensions but retained the platform design of the original line with a big station tunnel and narrow island platform in the middle of two running lines as seen here at Clapham North, along with Clapham Common. Back then, although patronage of the line was high, compared to today's volume, the narrowness of the platform could become hazardous during busy periods. Here we see a southbound train departing. (Friday 11 November 2016)

South Wimbledon is the penultimate stop before the line enters the open into Morden station. The extension produced some of Charles Holden's earliest classic forms of building work for the Underground. At street level, simple clean lined concrete buildings were built as the ticket offices with most of them being built on the corner sites of the street. On the platforms, a uniform design was provided throughout the extension, with the exception of the platforms at Clapham North and Clapham Common, of which an example can be seen here on the northbound platform, which does have a 1920s elegance to it, with the tile scheme and roundel sign raised high with a border around it. (Tuesday 22 November 2016)

Finchley Central was opened by the Great Northern Railway on 22 August 1867 under the name 'Finchley & Hendon'. It was later renamed 'Finchley' on 1 February 1872 and the track and platform layout was altered to allow trains to continue up to High Barnet. Further name changes to 'Finchley (Church End)' in 1894, and finally its current title Finchley Central on 1 April 1940. The Northern Line started running here on 14 April 1940 on the line's High Barnet extension and it is also the junction for the Mill Hill East branch, which currently runs in the off peak as a shuttle train between here and Mill Hill East. Great Northern Railway origins are still very much in evidence here with the station buildings and bridge over the tracks, seen in view as this train pulls in off the High Barnet branch led by 1995 Tube Stock 51535. This station was a theme for 1967 pop song *Finchley Central* by The New Vaudeville Band. (Sunday 11 December 2016)

There are a number of train stabling sidings alongside High Barnet station being visible from the platform; it was the scene of an incident on 7 August 1953, when a train of 1938 Tube Stock that was shunting over-ran the shunting neck with the leading car turning on its side down an embankment. This station was opened on 1 April 1872 and taken over by the Northern Line's electric trains on 14 April 1940. Thankfully, many of the stations up to High Barnet still retain architecture and buildings from steam days before the line was taken over by London Transport; as well as the station buildings retained here we can also see an old wooden framed Signal Cabin still in situ. The station retains a peaceful air to it as a train of 1995 Tube Stock takes rest before its next trundle back to Kennington via Charing Cross. Note the dot next to the car number of 51723 on the bottom left hand side of its cab, this denotes that this is a unit with equipment that releases de-icing fluid on the rails during snow and icy weather conditions. (Sunday 11 December 2016)

Camden Town boasts the most complex junction on the Underground network, with a number of running tunnels passing above and below each other in order to connect to and from either the Bank or Charing Cross branches, as well to the Edgware or High Barnet branches. There are four platforms altogether, two for the Edgware branch and two for the High Barnet branch. On 19 October 2003, a train derailed on a set of points here with the derailed car hitting the tunnel wall, the fifth car being partially derailed. The cause was said to be in the design of the point-work. Some years later, we see 1995 Tube Stock 51601 departing from the Edgware branch platforms for Kennington via Charing Cross. Trains serve both Kennington and Morden from both the High Barnet and Edgware branches from Camden Town. (Sunday 11 December 2016)

During the building of the Victoria Line, an opportunity was taken to create cross-platform interchange with the Northern Line at some stations, such as Highbury & Islington (then part of the Northern City Line), Stockwell, and here at Euston. Euston used to have a small island platform with both running lines either side in one tunnel, and with the coming of the Victoria Line, the northbound line was diverted into a new station tunnel and the track covered over causing this wider than usual platform with connecting corridors across to the new Victoria Line platform. Such wider platforms could be an advantage at many of the systems stations but sometimes it would take a lot of reconstruction and money to rebuild platforms to this size. Here, a train of 1995 Tube Stock has just off-loaded some of its passengers. (Sunday 11 December 2016)

Belsize Park is one of several stations on the Northern Line which had separate deep level air raid shelters built close to it. The other deep level shelters were located at Clapham South, Clapham Common, Clapham North, Stockwell, Goodge Street, and Camden Town. The Clapham South shelter was later re-used as a place to temporarily house some of the first Caribbean migrants who came to England on the SS *Windrush* in 1947, many of whom would later work for London Transport on the Underground and buses as well as British Rail. Most of the underground shelters and the white painted brick structures at street level remain visible and intact. Here 1995 Tube Stock 51524 departs. (Saturday 24 December 2016)

Holding the record for being the deepest tube station anywhere on the Underground network, Hampstead sits 192ft (58.5m) below ground level and is served by lifts. It was originally to be called Heath Street after the nearby street the station is located on, with the name being tiled onto the end of the platform, but Hampstead was chosen instead. There are five other Hampstead stations; London Overground has three of them at Hampstead Heath, West Hampstead, and South Hampstead. The others are West Hampstead Jubilee Line and West Hampstead Thameslink. 1995 Tube Stock 51544 leads its train into the station. (Saturday 24 December 2016)

The line interchanges with the Metropolitan, Hammersmith & City, and Circle lines here at Moorgate, as well as Great Northern services to Welwyn Garden City and Hertford North of which Mainline trains serve the former Northern City Line which used to operate between Moorgate and Finsbury Park. This station is well known to many for the tragic crash that occurred on the morning of 28 February 1975 during the morning rush hour, when a train failed to stop and continued beyond the platform into the short overrun tunnel in platform 9 compacting the first three cars of the train into the short space, sadly killing the driver and many of the passengers in the first few cars and causing injuries to the rest. Many precautions were taken after this incident with two trainstop devices being installed along the platform, so that a train cannot enter the platform and accelerate causing another incident. This Northern Line 1995 Tube Stock headed by 51553 enters on its way to High Barnet, and incidentally had London Transport's Northern Heights extensions had gone ahead, this train would be connecting at East Finchley with trains from Platform 9 and 10 today. (Sunday 1 January 2017)

When the City & South London Railway opened its line between King William Street and Stockwell, it did not serve London Bridge but with the construction of a new station at Bank, an opportunity was taken to open a new station at London Bridge too, opening on 25 February 1900. It sits between Bank and Borough stations and has interchange with the bus station above which has been on the station forecourt since the Mainline train station was opened here back in horse bus days. Unusually, the running lines are arranged into right hand running (like in Europe and America) due to the northbound line running east of the southbound line, instead of west of it between south of Borough and south of Moorgate. The coming of the Jubilee Line extension here saw the Northern platforms being rebuilt in the late 1990s, with a larger passageway between the running tunnels to allow greater circulation for the increase of passengers that the new extension was to generate here. (Sunday 1 January 2017)

The terminus at Edgware was opened on 18 August 1924, when the line was extended from Hendon Central, bringing new stations to the areas of Colindale and Burnt Oak which were just beginning to lose their acres of countryside to outer suburb housing estates. During the 1930s and '40s, London Transport planned new extensions and lines, with Edgware to become a through station on the line to Bushey Heath but because of the Second World War delaying the project and later Green belt regulations, the plans never materialised. This has left Edgware station looking as though it is an incomplete station. It has a three platform layout with the island platform beneath the train shed being where the through trains would have passed. Here we see a train of 1995 Tube Stock departing while two other trains wait their turn in the other platforms. (Saturday 7 January 2017)

Originally opened as 'Oxford Street' on 22 June 1907, the station was a year later renamed Tottenham Court Road on 9 March 1908 on the same day that the original Tottenham Court Road station was renamed to what we know today as Goodge Street station. This station at both platform and street level has seen huge redevelopment projects; many of the surrounding buildings were demolished, some of which were of historical interest, to accommodate the building of Crossrail through here. The original Central London Railway building was demolished and the various subways abandoned, with the building of a brand new station building on the corner of Charing Cross Road and Oxford Street and two new entrances near to the famous Centre Point building. A new sub-surface ticket hall area was built and many of the passageways rebuilt. At platform level, new tiling and signage has been put in place for the arrival of the new Elizabeth Line due to arrive here around 2019. The station will bring a huge increase of passengers on top of the large numbers this station already sees, such as the load that will disembark from this 1995 Tube Stock train with 51612 leading. (Sunday 22 January 2017)

Chapter 6

Bakerloo Line

The Bakerloo Line, like the District Line between Gunnersbury and Richmond, shares some of its tracks with London Overground north of Queen's Park. Here at Harrow & Wealdstone, we see a seven-car train of 1972 Tube Stock headed by 3537 having detrained its passengers, as it waits for the shunt signal into the reversing siding. Many of the passengers will wait for an onward service to Watford Junction operated by London Overground's Mainline stock. Until September 1982, passengers could have remained on a Bakerloo Line train continuing up to Watford Junction until service cuts saw it cut back to Stonebridge Park, although later extended to Harrow & Wealdstone. This stock is rumoured to be the last of London Underground stock to be withdrawn which date back to London Transport days. (Saturday 4 April 2015)

The 1972 Tube Stock was built in two batches; the Mk I version was built for the Northern Line to help replace some of the ageing 1938 Tube Stock and were very similar in appearance to the 1967 Tube Stock on the Victoria Line, with both being finished in all-over unpainted aluminium. The first train entered service on 26 June 1972, with a few Motor-trailer pairs later on in their life being incorporated into the 1967 Tube Stock fleet in the middle of the train formations and later into the 1972 Mk II Tube Stock batch. The second batch classified as Mk II now reside on the Bakerloo Line and had some minor differences, having an electronic train number box placed in the offside cab window as opposed to the plates inserted into the cab front door and having red painted car doors giving relief to the all unpainted aluminium finish. North Wembley on the 1917 extension sees motor car 3244 at the rear of this departing Harrow & Wealdstone train with a front cab 'M' door taken from a 1967/1972 Mk I Tube Stock train that makes it stand out from the other units, whilst a southbound train also departs from the other platform. (Sunday 26 June 2016)

Kenton is the penultimate stop on the Bakerloo Line before it finally completes its journey at Harrow & Wealdstone. Much of the original station and platform buildings remaining are now very old and need lots of repairs and works to them to keep them fit for service; here there is a temporary bridge over onto the southbound platform which looks very much an eyesore whilst works to demolish the old footbridge takes place and a new one built. A 1972 Tube Stock train headed by 3262 comes to a stop underneath the structure on its southbound journey to the Elephant. (Friday 11 November 2016)

The Bakerloo Line passes through Kensal Green tunnel between Kensal Green and Willesden Junction; although they look like tube tunnels, they are built to Mainline size to accommodate the Mainline trains to Watford Junction that also share the tracks. The Bakerloo was extended through here as far as Willesden Junction on 10 May 1915 in a joint scheme with the London & North Western Railway. Here, on a cold misty December morning a 1972 Tube Stock train leaves the tunnel with 3267 leading a southbound train into the platform for Elephant & Castle. (Thursday 1 December 2016)

Baker Street Bakerloo Line station opened on 10 March 1906 (the Metropolitan Railway station opened here in 1863) as the northern terminus of the Baker Street & Waterloo Railway. A few weeks later, on 27 March 1906, it was extended a further stop to Great Central later renamed Marylebone on 15 April 1917, where it interchanged with London's last Mainline terminus to be built. When the Bakerloo took over the branch to Stanmore, the new tunnels to Finchley Road opened on 20 November 1939 and necessitated the building of an additional southbound platform here. During the 1980s, the platform walls received new tiling with the use of small Sherlock Holmes motifs making up one large Sherlock Holmes smoking a pipe, as seen here and continued at various points along the platform. (Friday 2 December 2016)

Regent's Park has no station building and has a sub-surface ticket hall where lifts take you down to the platforms; north and southbound platforms are placed one above the other instead of the traditional style of side by side in separate tunnels. Here we can see the original tiles with some of the damaged ones being replaced with exact replicas during the station's refurbishment. It is one of the stations in the vicinity for London Zoo and Regent's Park but for a zone 1 station is not overly busy. (Friday 2 December 2016)

Elephant & Castle today is the southern terminus of the Bakerloo Line and was extended here from Waterloo on 5 August 1906, having a separate station building from the Northern Line one that was opened on 18 December 1890 by the City & South London Railway. At platform level, passengers can interchange below ground between lines using the connecting subway tunnels. The line was to be further extended to Camberwell Green with the tunnelling already begun but the Second World War halted the plans and for many years after the war the extension was still on the tube map as under construction until it finally disappeared. In recent years, the plan has been brought back to life with talks of extending the line down to the Bromley and Hayes areas. Should the extension come to fruition, new rolling stock would be ordered for the line, bringing an end to the hard-working 1972 Tube Stock such as 3253 slowly pulling into platform 3 to take a short rest before it heads back north on another trip. (Friday 2 December 2016)

The Bakerloo Line interchanges with the Central & Victoria lines and provides cross platform interchange with the Victoria Line at Oxford Circus. The Central arrived here first in 1900, the Bakerloo in 1906 and the Victoria Line in 1969 and is one of the system's busiest stations today, serving the famous shopping street at Oxford Street. 1972 Tube Stock 3247 departs on a northbound train. (Saturday 24 December 2016)

The Bakerloo Line has a separate station of the same name at Edgware Road as the District, Circle, and Hammersmith & City Line station located nearby. The station retains its elegant Leslie Green station building situated on the corner of the Edgware and Marylebone Roads. This station received refurbishment work in the 1990s but thankfully retained much of the style of the original station using the same colour scheme tiles and even re-introducing the old style hexagonal light shade fittings. This station is also one of several to retain replicas of the original wall name panels within the tile work at the end of the platforms. A 1972 Tube Stock closes its doors to depart for Harrow & Wealdstone. (Saturday 24 December 2016)

At Queen's Park, the line emerges into the open and climbs a subtle gradient up into the station where cross platform interchange is provided with the Euston to Watford Junction Line operated by London Overground. To the north of the platform are four car sheds with the outer two being used during service hours as the northbound and southbound through tracks and the middle two are used to reverse terminating trains, with a further two stabling sheds to the south of the station. Bakerloo Line trains are able to use the Overground lines between here and Kilburn High Road to reverse in time of disruption or engineering works should the need occur and provides a rare sight. A 1972 Tube Stock lead by 3258 departs the shed on a service back to Elephant & Castle while another train waits in the platform to stable in one of the sheds. (Saturday 24 December 2016)

Harlesden was opened on 15 June 1912, with Bakerloo services starting here on 16 April 1917. It was once served by a second station nearby opened by the Midland Railway situated on the Dudding Hill Line which is now a freight only line but was closed to passenger trains in 1902. Two trains of 1972 Tube Stock pass as they enter and leave the station. (Saturday 24 December 2016)

'MIND THE GAP'. Many of the early tube lines followed the geography of the roads above and had to twist and curve to avoid building under developments above so that money did not have to be paid to property owners as compensation for having a railway line rumbling beneath their property and to pay for strengthening of the properties foundations. This in turn caused some stations to have very curved platforms like this, causing some very big gaps when stepping between train and platform. This later lead to the familiar announcement 'Mind the gap' that is known worldwide as well as by the many generations of Londoners who use the Underground. The Bakerloo is a line that has a lot of twists and turns on its route and here, a train of 1972 Tube Stock has just off-loaded at Waterloo on its way to Elephant & Castle, with the gap evident. (Saturday 24 December 2016)

The Bakerloo Line serves four Mainline termini along its route at Waterloo, Charing Cross, Marylebone and here at Paddington, where it also interchanges with the District and Circle lines at the station, and the Hammersmith & City and Circle lines that serve a separate station alongside the actual Mainline station. This station was opened on 1 December 1913 and is seeing a considerable amount of works taking place in connection with the Crossrail line which will interchange and come to the surface here, bringing a huge increase in passengers passing through here over the amount this busy station already handles. A train of 1972 Tube Stock gets ready to depart for Elephant & Castle. (Wednesday 4 January 2017)

Piccadilly Circus station on the Bakerloo Line is unusual in that, not only is it not built to traditional island platform layout, but you are able to see either northbound or southbound trains enter and depart the station at the northern end of either platforms, where there is also a crossover allowing southbound trains to reverse to the northbound track. This station was largely reconstructed in the 1920s, to cope with the heavy flow of passengers. The new station reopened on 10 December 1928, designed by Charles Holden. This station no longer has street level buildings with passengers descending the many subways of the circus to a sub-surface ticketing facilities. Here a train of 1972 Tube Stock has just off-loaded some passengers many of whom are tourists who will go to see the Eros statue and the large TV screens and lights. (Sunday 15 January 2017)

Chapter 7

Piccadilly Line

On the morning of Monday 2 February 2009, the whole of London & the South East of Britain woke to a thick fall of snow which kept on throughout the day. Here at Northfields, we see a train of 1973 Tube Stock departing for Heathrow Terminals 1, 2, 3 & 5 as another waits to depart for Central London. The system was severely disrupted due to the snowfall and overcrowding at stations due to delays and limited service of trains, however, credit and thanks must go to the staff who also must have struggled to get in and who tried their best to provide as good a service they could for their passengers. (Monday 2 February 2009)

The Uxbridge branch is shared with the Metropolitan Line and at Ruislip Manor; here, two trains of 1973 Tube Stock pass each other with the train on the right on its long journey from Uxbridge to Cockfosters. In 2005, this station was modernised with platforms being rebuilt and new canopies added towards the middle of the platform complementing the shorter older canopies at the western end of the platform and installations as seen here. This stock is now the second oldest in service on the Underground. (Wednesday 16 November 2011)

A blanket of thick fog surrounds this train of 1973 Tube Stock as it enters Acton Town. This station has a four-platform layout, the middle two for the Piccadilly and the outer two for the District, although the Piccadilly Line often uses all four. The Piccadilly Line was extended to here in 1932, when the track between Hammersmith and Acton Town was quadrupled and the platforms were rebuilt from three to four configuration. The Piccadilly Line has stabling sidings here to the east of the station with one to the west. The track from the right comes from Acton Works where heavy engineering works to trains and various other works takes place that cannot be done in any of the Underground lines depots. (Sunday 20 November 2011)

Over the Christmas period of 2013, the District and Piccadilly lines saw engineering work over various parts of its routes, which saw certain Piccadilly Line trains providing a frequent service on the District Line between Hammersmith and Ealing Broadway, serving all the stations in between while still providing the non-stop run between Hammersmith and Acton Town. Here, we see a 1973 Tube Stock train departing platform 8 at Ealing Broadway usually served by trains of D Stock. This stock has occasionally served these District platforms in the past, when football special trains were often put on in the 1970/80s. (Friday 27 December 2013)

In the 1990s, Hammersmith District & Piccadilly Line station was completely rebuilt to a more modern design, losing its 1930s rebuilt platform canopies and fittings. Its street level building, which gave it character from times past, was incorporated into a newly built shopping centre. Here we see a Piccadilly Line train crawling in after its non-stop run between Acton Town and this station on its journey to Cockfosters. These trains had recently had new dot matrix destination indicators installed, which can be seen here clearly. Hammersmith was the line's terminus from its opening in 1906 until 1932 when the line was extended westwards. (Saturday 3 October 2015)

A 1973 Tube Stock train passes through Stamford Brook at speed with motor car 127 leading, where the Piccadilly Line is only able to serve this station on the westbound track if the need should arise. The platform to the trains left is the eastbound District Line platform. (Saturday 3 October 2015)

At Boston Manor, a train tailed by 229 departs towards its next station at Northfields. This train will now run alongside the site of Northfields depot which spans between here and the station of the same name. To the right of the westbound platform is a depot shunt track and a track where trains can enter and leave the depot from the Heathrow end. Note the platform canopies at the far end of the platform, dating back to when the District Railway opened the branch. Not many of today's Piccadilly Line passengers realise that this branch was once a part of the District, with trains still serving it to Hounslow West up until 1964, long before the line was diverted to a new station built underground and on to the now expansive Heathrow Airport. (Sunday 1 November 2015)

Covent Garden was opened on 11 April 1907. This station retains its name signs incorporated into the wall tiling at both ends of the platform, along with an example of the early bullseye roundel first introduced in 1908. Covent Garden is the station you alight for the London Transport Museum, so it is a nice touch that this particular station would have lots of its original fittings still in place, including its distinctive tiling colour scheme from opening so that passengers could recognise their station due to the names only being displayed at each end of the platforms. (Tuesday 17 November 2015)

Sudbury Town used to be a station on the District Railway, with a shuttle service provided between South Harrow and Mill Hill Park, the latter being renamed Acton Town when the Piccadilly Line was extended and took over this branch in 1932. As the stations and tracks were already here on the branch, the London Passenger Transport Board rebuilt most of the stations and infrastructure to more modern standards, as can be seen the footbridge and ticket booking hall built in an art deco style popular of the time by Charles Holden. These buildings and structures still look as modern, sleek and clean today as they did when new back then, as we see a 1973 Tube Stock train lead by 127 come to a stop on its long journey to Cockfosters. (Sunday 21 February 2016)

Under the watchful eye of the art deco booking hall at Oakwood, the Night Tube liveried 1973 Tube Stock train enters its first stop after leaving Cockfosters, on its way to Heathrow Terminals 1, 2, 3 & 5. These 1930s stations, with their magnificent booking halls, look even more impressive at night under the lights. Cockfosters Depot is accessed by trains to the left and occupies a large site between here and Cockfosters. This station was originally called Enfield West when it opened but was renamed Oakwood. (Sunday 21 February 2016)

At Hounslow Central, we see the Night Tube advert train again, this time heading back to Cockfosters having made its journey to Heathrow Terminals 1, 2, 3 & 5. The Heathrow branch generally gets a train every five minutes for the obvious reason that it serves Heathrow Airport. The 1973 Tube Stock depicted here were specially built for the Heathrow extension and entered service between 1975 and 1979, consisting of 87½ six-car trains, replacing some trains of seven-car 1938 Tube Stock and its main fleet of seven-car 1956/59 Tube Stock. One unit was scrapped in recent times due to it being involved in the very sad 7/7 bombing at Russell Square back in 2005. (Sunday 21 February 2016)

Turnham Green is a District Line station but is served by Piccadilly Line trains early morning and late evenings. Piccadilly Line trains sometimes serve here during the day if there is engineering work on the District Line or if there is severe disruption, but on this occasion the service is good as this train thunders through towards Hammersmith. The eastbound platforms were once served by the London & South Western Railway, which operated through here from Richmond to a spur at Hammersmith connecting onto the Hammersmith & City Line. The remains of the viaduct between Ravenscourt Park and Hammersmith can still be seen from the trains. (Tuesday 26 July 2016)

Between the complete opening of the full length of the Victoria Line and the opening of the Jubilee Line, the Piccadilly Line's Heathrow extension was the newest section of Underground line to be constructed opening in stages; it is still growing today with the latest station at Heathrow Terminal 5. The usual construction method for a tube line was not used on the extension, with the earlier method of cut and cover construction being used, where a deep trench was dug out just below ground level, the necessary wall structure etc being built, then being roofed over. The station seen here at Hounslow West replaced the original station opened by the District Railway in 1884 under the name of Hounslow Barracks, renamed in 1925. The original platforms were located where today's station car park stands and received a Charles Holden station building, which thankfully was kept when the new station was opened in 1975. (Sunday 23 October 2016)

Opened on 19 July 1975, Hatton Cross remained the terminus for over two years until Heathrow Central was opened (later renamed Heathrow Airport Terminals 1, 2, 3 in 1983), with all three stations of the new extension looking similar in design but with minor differences unique to each station. Here a train departs to Heathrow Terminals 1, 2, 3 & 5, and it will diverge here from the loop line which serves Terminal 4 then back to Terminals 1, 2, & 3 where the trains then proceed back to Central London. (Sunday 23 October 2016)

Due to the station being on a single clockwise loop, Heathrow Terminal 4 station was built with only one platform, where trains would continue clockwise to terminate in either one of the two platforms at Heathrow Terminals 1, 2, & 3, where trains would wait for a few minutes before departing back to Central London. This station opened nine years after the original Heathrow extension on 12 April 1986 and still retains a clean fresh look thirty years later in 2016, as demonstrated with this 1973 Tube Stock train, awaiting its departure time back to Central London. (Sunday 23 October 2016)

The station at Osterley lies approximately 300m to the south west of the original opened in 1883 by the District Railway named Osterley & Spring Grove. The current station opened on 25 March 1934, with the street level building marking a new standard of design by architect Charles Holden, contrasting greatly from his more usual box and drum shaped buildings from the two previous years Piccadilly extensions. Here, a train pulls in on its journey into Central London passing a Heathrow bound train just seen in the distance departing. (Friday 4 October 2016)

After leaving Park Royal, the line climbs and once reaching Alperton, the line is running on a viaduct above the rooftops. The station was built to art deco style and fits in with the design of the nearby Alperton bus garage, which also was built to the same style. Alperton usually has a number of passengers waiting on the platforms but due to faults with the 1973 Tube Stocks wheel sets, many trains were out of service having the faults corrected leaving most of the serviceable trains to serve the Heathrow branch, with a limited shuttle between Acton Town and Rayners Lane and rail replacement buses also helping out. A train of 1973 Tube Stock departs on one such shuttle train towards Acton Town. (Thursday 8 December 2016)

Ealing Common is a shared District/Piccadilly Line station on the Ealing Broadway/Uxbridge branches. Many trains on the Uxbridge branch reverse at Rayners Lane, leaving the Uxbridge branch mainly to be served by the Metropolitan Line with which it shares the branch. This station was also rebuilt to Charles Holden's Art deco style of the 1930s as can be seen from the concrete platform canopies and the station building above with its glass windows with the roundel incorporated. Stations that are shared between tube and surface lines often leave a big step up or down between train and platform. Here, the station building above and the platforms are seen to good effect, as the all over Night Tube advert train motors out on the Acton Town to Rayners Lane shuttle service. (Thursday 8 December 2016)

The Second World War and especially the Blitz of 1940/1941 and the V weapons of the latter part of the war brought a lot of destruction to Britain's cities with London being one of the worst affected. During the 1950s and 1960s, many old buildings, sometimes of very great architectural value, were torn down and new concrete box building replaced them, leading to a movement which is still going on today which gets such buildings a listed status by the Secretary of State and the National Heritage, meaning they cannot be knocked down or altered. A train of 1973 Tube Stock departs Turnpike Lane station – given Grade II listed status in 1994 – for Heathrow Terminals 1, 2, 3 & 5. It retains its bus station above, connecting with the many routes serving across North London and it is proposed that an interchange here will be provided by Crossrail 2 on its Cheshunt branch. (Saturday 24 December 2016)

Wood Green station was also given Grade II listed status in July 2011 and has an unusual station building design from the rest in that it is incorporated into the street corner, sandwiched between a row of shops on Lordship Lane and Green Lanes at Jolly Butchers Hill. The extension brought much development in the 1930s, turning fields and farmland into bustling suburban High Streets as in Wood Green today. On 16 March 1976, an IRA bomb that went off the day after the West Ham incident mentioned in the District Line chapter, went off here, when a bomb on an empty train of 1959 Tube Stock waiting in the platform prematurely detonated at around 21:15 in one of the cars towards the centre of the train. One passenger waiting on the platform was injured by the glass sent flying and this could have been a more tragic event, had the bomb not detonated prematurely; the train was about to run empty to pick up home-going football supporters from Arsenal! (Saturday 24 December 2016)

The Underground suffered some major destruction during the Second World War; Bounds Green was a casualty on the night of 13 October 1940 during the heavy Blitz on London when a lone German aircraft dropped a bomb on some houses to the north of the station where people were taking refuge during an air raid. The damage from the houses caused the north end of the northbound platform tunnel to collapse, killing and injuring many of those sheltering on the platforms and disrupting services for two months while the rubble was cleared and repairs made. There is a plaque on the platform commemorating the lives lost on that day, and the station would survive the war to become Grade II listed in January 2010. A 1973 Tube Stock train coasts in on its way to Cockfosters. (Saturday 24 December 2016)

Southgate is often widely regarded as one of Charles Holden's finest pieces of work on the Piccadilly Line's extensions of the 1930s and even ranks highly in the list of the most important 1930s public buildings within London. The station building occupies a small elliptical island separated from the main shopping arcade with a slip road for buses only to serve the station. Passengers have an unusual view at platform level in that you are able to be below ground on a tube line and be able to see daylight at the end of the tunnel, as can be seen here in this view. (Saturday 24 December 2016)

Cockfosters is the line's northern terminus with trains reaching here on 31 July 1933 and opened under the newly formed London Passenger Transport Board, which under act of Parliament absorbed all of London's Underground Railways, Trams, Trolleybuses, and buses under one ownership ridding London of many individual pirate companies on 1 July 1933. It has this magnificent concrete train shed that spans all three tracks which the design of Uxbridge at the other end of the line was influenced by pretty much having the same design and layout. The station building situated on Cockfosters Road was built in a modern European style using brick, glass, and reinforced concrete with passengers descending stairs to a ticket office at platform level. This station retains much of its historical artefacts with the station receiving Grade II listed status. Two trains of 1973 Tube Stock wait their turns to depart on their long runs west. Trains run alongside the depot of the same name between here and Oakwood. Saturday 24 December 2016.

Arnos Grove is situated in the London Borough of Enfield and acted as the line's temporary northern terminus between 19 September 1932 and 13 March 1933, when the line was extended to Oakwood (opened as Enfield West), one stop short of its target at Cockfosters. There are three platforms here, with trains often terminating and reversing in the middle platform helping to provide a frequent service through the Central London section, with one such train seen departing in the distance while another pauses as drivers change over on its run to Cockfosters. To the west of the station there are a number of stabling sidings and a large train crew depot. This station was given Grade II listed status on 19 February 1971 and received a refurbishment in 2005 but maintaining its heritage features and fixtures. In July 2011, Arnos Grove's listed status was upgraded to Grade I*. (Saturday 24 December 2016)

Three lines all converge on Gloucester Road with the District & Circle lines at sub-surface level and the Piccadilly Line at tube level which is accessed by lifts from the ticket hall. The Piccadilly Line platforms were opened on 15 December 1906 at the same time that the station was renamed from Brompton (Gloucester Road) to Gloucester Road. This station oozes with history with many of its signs, tiling, and architecture retained. Here, we see a 1973 Tube Stock train arriving for Rayners Lane. (Sunday 1 January 2017)

The station at Holborn was opened by the Great Northern, Piccadilly & Brompton Railway on the 15 December 1906, a few hundred yards from the Central London Railway's station at British Museum situated on High Holborn. In 1932/33, new platforms were being constructed at Holborn for the Central Line to provide interchange between the two lines and the building works such as building the platform tunnels took place while the service trains were still running, something unthinkable today! The old station at British Museum closed on 24 September 1933 and the new platforms opened the following day, with both lines serving the same station just as they do today. Both lines received a platform refurbishment in the 1980s which used panels displaying images of various artefacts from the nearby British Museum, such as mummies, marble floor patterns, and various stonework exhibits. Such an example can be seen here with the twin pillars predominantly found in the surviving buildings of Ancient Kemet (Egypt) and Ancient Greece, as a train of 1973 Tube Stock departs in the distance. (Sunday 15 January 2017)

Chapter 8

Central Line

In 2012, the switchover of all television sets from analogue channels to digital took place. A whole train of 1992 Tube Stock was given an all-over advert to promote this and here at Barkingside we see 91055 leading the train into the Countrified LNER built station with much of its original features retained. Most of the stations on the eastern end of the Central Line beyond Leyton were originally owned and served by LNER trains out into the Essex countryside, and it still feels very weird today travelling at speed on a tube train in the open countryside up to Epping. This train is heading for Ealing Broadway. (Saturday 18 February 2012)

Here we see a close up of the advert vinyl applied to the car sides and doors. (Saturday 18 February 2012)

Holland Park received upgrade work in 2016, with some of the station's old signage being replaced with modern examples and receiving some new wall tiling on the platforms and passageways. Before the long term closure for refurbishment of the lifts, platforms and passageways, we see a very empty platform on the first day of the New Year. The station name and line frieze signage has been retained, but the large 1960s name signs have since been replaced by modern versions. Euston square also has this style name and line frieze signage. (Friday 1 January 2016)

Greenford station has an unusual platform layout with the Central Line serving the two outer tracks of an island platform and a single Mainline track in the middle used by DMU trains operated by Great Western trains, on the branch between here and West Ealing. Here we see a train lead by 91107 coming to a stop on its long run to Epping which from West Ruislip is the longest continuous journey on the Underground at 34.1 miles. Between West Ruislip and North Acton, the Central Line runs parallel to Chiltern Railways into Marylebone and a freight line, to the left of this 1992 Tube Stock can be seen an example of two now rare semaphore signals especially for the London area; they do however still exist on the Mainline network in various places. (Saturday 2 July 2016)

Most of the Central Line's stations east of Leyton, except for the Underground section between Leytonstone and Newbury Park, were former Great Eastern Railway lines and Fairlop is one of the stations on the Hainault branch that has kept its original buildings and most notable at this station is the original glass windows of the waiting room, still with the old writing in situ. A 1992 Tube Stock train sits in the platform with car 91047 nearest. (Friday 14 October 2016)

During the Second World War, London Transport and its staff helped contribute significantly towards the war effort by using their various Road and Rail works to build and assemble weapons, components and even fighter planes. One of the more obscure locations was the new Central Line tunnels, which would have had tube trains running through them at the time but the war came and extensions were delayed. A factory producing aircraft components was set up by the Plessey Company between Leytonstone and Gants Hill, covering nearly five miles of railway tunnels and having its own little narrow gauge railway, with machinery all crammed into the small tunnel space where it was protected from the air raids above. It would have been a location least thought to have a factory by spies for the enemy. After the war, the Central Line extensions progressed, with this station winning a design award; Stalin adopted the design for the new Moscow Metro. Most of the new stations on the extension boasted modern fluorescent lighting. A train departs Gants Hill for Central London. (Friday 18 November 2016)

Hainault is the location of the Central Line's eastern depot and is situated on the entire site between Grange Hill and Hainault. Most of the stations between Newbury Park to Hainault and round the loop to Woodford were still steam operated prior to the Central Line extension here on the branch from Ilford. The line was electrified as far as here in May 1948 and six months later electric trains continued round to Woodford. The island platform 1 and 2 depicted here received this concrete waiting room and canopy and the concrete lamp post and station name structure. The westbound platform 3 retains its Great Eastern Railway origins structure and canopy. (Friday 18 November 2016)

Buckhurst Hill is located adjacent to the northern boundary of Greater London and forms part of the Greater London Urban Area. The railway line was opened by the Eastern Counties Railway in 1856 and to this day remains a very much middle class development. Before the railway line was built, the town was on a stagecoach route between London and Cambridge, Norwich, Bury St Edmunds, and Dunmow. The railways helped immensely with the housing development of the area with Chingford station also not too far away on a branch into Liverpool Street, serving the inner suburbs of the Walthamstow and Hackney areas now operated by London Overground. Here we see 91103 entering the station on its journey into Central London, with a very nicely kept Great Eastern Railway footbridge across the tracks to the westbound platform in the background. (Tuesday 21 November 2016)

From 21 November 1948, Loughton was the limit of electrification for the Central Line, being extended from Woodford on the same day as its extensions in the west, until 25 September 1949, when the line was further electrified and extended to Epping. The little over six miles single track branch between Epping and Ongar continued to be worked by the vintage LNER steam trains however when electrification began in 1956, with the first electric train taking over from steam trains on 18 November 1957. To the west of the station there are a number of stabling sidings and a three platform layout built entirely in a still very clean and modern looking unique art deco style. A train of 1992 Tube Stock sits in the platform waiting to depart for West Ruislip as dusk creeps in. (Tuesday 21 November 2016)

Epping today is the line's eastern terminus and is one of eight London Underground stations located in the Epping Forest District of Essex. It retains its atmosphere of a little country station and it is well patronised by passengers and was the one-time terminus of its Epping to Ongar shuttle service, which used to terminate in the platform the train is sitting in this view. The line up to Ongar covered just over six miles, serving two intermediate stations at North Weald and Blake Hall (closed in 1981) due to the lowest amount of passenger usage anywhere on the Underground; the line faced threats of closure many times throughout the 1970s and 1980s. The line finally succumbed to the axe on 30 September 1994 on the same day that the Aldwych branch of the Piccadilly Line closed. When the Central Line served the branch it brought the lines mileage to 51¼ miles and made it the longest of the Underground lines with much of it in the open. The Underground measured its distances from Ongar at mile post 0.0. The branch can be travelled on today as it has reopened as a preserved railway line by the Epping Ongar Railway and perhaps sometime in the near future the railway would be authorised to connect at Epping with the Central Line as it once did. (Tuesday 21 November 2016)

Theydon Bois is situated amongst green fields and is a lovely little village located in Essex. It lies on the edge of the vast Epping Forest and has a unique characteristic of not having any street lighting to preserve its country village characteristics. Waiting for a train at this station can be very tranquil but the peace was soon to be disturbed when this 1962 Tube Stock 'Rail Adhesion Train' led by car 1406 rumbled through its old haunt causing loads of noise with its wheel flats. The 1962 Tube Stock was specially ordered for the Central Line and was quite similar to the Piccadilly Line's 1959 Tube Stock. The last fifty-seven trains of 1959 Tube Stock for the Piccadilly were diverted to the Central on a temporary basis until the 1962 Tube Stock were delivered, due to the line's Standard Stock of 1920s vintage towards the end of its working life suffering a continuing large number of defects, necessitating the urgent need to replace them as quickly as possible. The first train of 1962 Tube Stock entered service on the 12 April 1962, with the last train operating the line on 17 February 1995 when the 1992 Tube Stock replaced them, eliminating the guards from this line. The 1959 Tube Stock and its guards survived a few years longer into the new millennium when the last train ran on 27 January 2000 on the Northern Line. (Tuesday 21 November 2016)

The Central Line's eastern and western extensions were delayed due to the Second World War, much of the resources and workforce being turned to the war effort. Bethnal Green station, like many Underground stations during the war, was used by civilians to shelter from the heavy bombing raids on London. Many of the local East Londoners took shelter here and an incident took place on the evening of the 3 March 1943 at 8:17pm. The air raid siren had sounded and people were entering the shelter in a calm manner. Blackout restrictions imposed restricted dim lighting and the Home Guard were testing a new defence gun in nearby Victoria Park, startling people, making them panic and start pushing to enter the shelter faster. A woman carrying a small child tripped on the dimly lit stairs and the people behind her starting to trip over her becoming trapped in the restricted space causing many to die from suffocation. This is thought to be the largest single loss of life during wartime in the UK during World War II that did not directly involve enemy action. A train of 1992 Tube Stock waits to depart westwards. (Wednesday 30 November 2016)

The Central London Railway (Central Line) was extended to Ealing Broadway from its terminus at Wood Lane (later replaced by White City) on 3 August 1920 and used the Great Western Railway station adjacent to that of the District Line. Both the Central and District have always used separate platforms here but for many years there was a physical connection between the two tracks; in recent years the connection has been removed. A train of 1992 Tube Stock sits in the platform awaiting the green signal to Hainault, whilst a train of S Stock can be seen waiting in one of the District platforms; of note is the train shed roof still in situ over the platforms dating from 1879. The wires for the Mainline trains can also been glimpsed on the left. (Wednesday 21 December 2016)

West of North Acton the West Ruislip and Ealing branches diverge using a flyover and dive-under. The eastbound platform was rebuilt to accommodate a third platform which was decommissioned previously in the past, allowing trains to be reversed here if need be whilst still allowing trains to pass undisrupted. A train of 1992 Tube Stock departs with 91031 on the rear. (Wednesday 21 December 2016)

London Transport originally planned to extend to Denham in Buckinghamshire but West Ruislip is as far as the line reached and is still the line's terminus today. It was originally opened as 'Ruislip & Ickenham' on 2 April 1906 by the Great Western & Great Central Joint Committee, later renamed West Ruislip (for Ickenham) on 30 June 1947, losing its suffix a little time later. The Central Line platforms were built in time for opening on 21 November 1948 and Mainline trains still serve this station on services into Marylebone and up to High Wycombe and Banbury with the occasionally diverted Great Western trains into Paddington. The line's western end depot is situated here with a connection to Mainline tracks, allowing trains to be delivered here for commissioning, or to be taken away by rail for scrapping or alterations at the various rail factories. There is also a single track line that connects to the Metropolitan and Piccadilly lines. (Wednesday 21 December 2016)

Northolt was opened on 21 November 1948 when the line was extended from Greenford and replaced an earlier station opened by the Great Western Railway in 1907, which closed when the new Central Line station opened. This station for many years had a temporary building which lasted for more than a decade after the new station opened, finally receiving its new building in around 1960, which still stands today. To the west of the station, a turn back siding is in situ, providing another convenient place to reverse late running trains. A train of 1992 Tube Stock accelerates at speed out of the station on its long run to Epping with 91103 on the rear. (Wednesday 21 December 2016)

Dusk starts to creep over London as this 1992 Tube Stock train led by 91069 pulls into Grange Hill, with a Woodford to Ealing Broadway service via Hainault. This station was opened in 1903 by the Great Eastern Railway on one of its branches between Woodford and Ilford, which ceased with the coming of the Central Line extension here on 21 November 1948. This section of track between Woodford and Hainault was part of the early experiment with Automatic Train Operation which was to later be used for the new Victoria Line. Some prototype trains were built and fitted with the same train equipment that the 1967 Tube Stock ordered for the Victoria Line would have. These prototype trains were classified as 1960 Tube Stock and would end their days plying the Epping to Ongar branch with, at the time of writing, a unit in preservation by the Cravens Heritage Trains and a unit that was converted to the Track Recording Train with a specially adapted 1973 Tube Stock trailer car inserted in the middle. (Thursday 22 December 2016)

Bank was opened on 30 July 1900 as the Central London Railway's terminus where it connected with the City & South London Railway and the London & South Western Railway's only tube line, the Waterloo & City Line. The line is under the same ownership as the Central Line today. The Docklands Light Railway also provides interchange with the Underground here since 1991 and this station sees a high flow of passengers from all the lines serving here, including those using the connection between the District and Circle lines at Monument. During the Second World War on 11 January 1941 during the height of the blitz on London, 111 people were killed when a German bomb penetrated the road junction above and crashed through the roof of the sub surface booking hall, leaving a huge crater in the middle of the road. The station remained closed for two months while repairs took place. Here we see the tightly curved platform which was curved sharply to avoid the line being built under the Bank of England above. (Saturday 7 January 2017)

Chapter 9

Waterloo & City Line

The Waterloo & City Line is a small self-contained line being only 1½ miles long and serving only two stations between Waterloo south of the River Thames and Bank to the north of it in the City, with no intermediate stops. The line was opened in 1898 by the Waterloo & City Railway and later became part of the London & South Western Railway, as a way of getting its passengers, many of them bankers and businessmen who travelled into London on their steam train services, across to the City but who had to continue their journey by other means. So the railway constructed this short line beneath the river to Bank, where their passengers could access the City quicker than the walking or the slow congested journey by horse bus/cab. Here at Waterloo, the small line has a small maintenance depot where minor work is carried out and where there are a small number of sidings which service trains use to reverse after detraining in one platform or to enter into another platform, as seen here, to pick up passengers to travel back to Bank. (Wednesday 4 January 2017)

Until 1994, this line was owned by British Rail using Southern Railway all-steel cars given the classification 1940 Stock, replacing the original wooden bodied cars operating the line since opening. These were later replaced by a small order of 1992 Tube Stock which was also ordered for the Central Line with the new trains replacing the final train of the old rolling stock on 28 May 1993; under British Rail's numbering system these were classified as the Class 482. Being completely self-contained and completely underground, the only means of getting rolling stock in and out of the line is by a hydraulic car lift, which necessitates the closing of the nearby streets. There was a plan to extend the line on numerous occasions but this did not materialise. The next train to depart waits in the platform at Bank. (Wednesday 4 January 2017)

Chapter 10

Jubilee Line

The Jubilee Line was originally to be named the Fleet Line; however, whilst being built the plan was for the line to be completed by 1977, the same year as HM Queen Elizabeth II Silver Jubilee, hence it was called Jubilee Line to commemorate this, though it did not actually open until two years later. The line was officially opened on 30 April 1979 by HRH Prince Charles, Prince of Wales, travelling between Charing Cross and Green Park with passenger services starting on the whole line to Stanmore from 1 May 1979. There were many different extension schemes planned for the line after that, to South-East London where the Underground has not really ventured into, but its current alignment through Docklands to Stratford was the final decision, opening in phases. Here at Stratford, which opened in phase one on Friday 14 May 1999 between here and North Greenwich, the LT Museum ran a railtour to celebrate thirty years of the Jubilee Line, using its preserved 1938 Tube Stock unit which, incidentally, operated the branch to Stanmore when it was part of the Bakerloo Line. (Wednesday 5 August 2009)

2012 was a hectic year for London as not only was it hosting the 2012 Olympics, it was also celebrating the Queen's Diamond Jubilee. In the Queen's Golden Jubilee year in 2002, Transport for London had painted fifty of its buses gold, just as it had painted twenty-five Routemaster buses silver for her Silver Jubilee in 1977. To celebrate her Diamond year, London Underground wrapped two trains of 1996 Tube Stock in a special vinyl all over advert as seen here in this view at Canons Park. It consisted of the Union Jack flag; a motif designed by some school children added a nice touch and a change from the usual corporate livery. (Saturday 5 June 2012)

West Hampstead has a mixed heritage, retaining its 1898 station building at street level and having a 1930s art deco design platform waiting room and canopy both seen in the distance here. The coming of the line here was a big operation for the engineers in 1938, as they had to re-organise the track layout into its present form between Finchley Road and Wembley Park. Here at West Hampstead, over the weekend of Saturday/Sunday 17/18 September 1938, the platform had to be moved sideways at a space of approximately ten feet, with the old track removed and new track laid; such a task seems unthinkable to be completed in the space of a weekend! The Jubilee Line provides the stopping service between Finchley Road and Wembley Park with Metropolitan Line trains providing a fast non-stop run. There are three stations all named West Hampstead and are all in close proximity of each other: the Jubilee Line station; London Overground's North London Line station; and National Rail's Thameslink station. (Thursday 13 October 2016)

The Stanmore branch was extended from Wembley Park by the Metropolitan Railway opening on 10 December 1932. Most of the station's buildings on the branch are built to Metropolitan Railway architecture, however the platform buildings such as here at Queensbury are very evident of 1930s art deco style. The stations are very basic but are very clean and attractive to look at and do what they were built to do. Here, a train of 1996 Tube Stock pulls into the platform, with 96019 leading a service to North Greenwich. Crossovers are provided at Waterloo, London Bridge and Canary Wharf, with crossovers providing access to the reversal platform at North Greenwich, designed with a three platform layout so that certain trains can be terminated in the timetable and during disruption and late running here just as at West Hampstead, Willesden Green, and Wembley Park. (Thursday 13 October 2016)

In the previous shot, a downpour was evident but at Stanmore, not a drop of rain. The station's Metropolitan Railway building can be seen in the background over-looking the train in the platform. Stanmore originally was built with only two platforms and in 2005 Transport for London started construction of a third platform, seen on the left of the picture. It was structurally completed in the summer of 2009 but was not actually put into use until the line's signalling upgrade was completed in July 2011, allowing more trains to run more frequently, at higher speeds under Automatic Train Operation. Stanmore has ten stabling sidings next to the right of the train and are all visible from the platform. (Thursday 13 October 2016)

Baker Street provides cross-platform interchange between the Bakerloo and Jubilee lines and has many platforms, with two on the Bakerloo, two on the Jubilee, two for the Hammersmith & City and Circle lines and four for the Metropolitan Line, it can get very busy when trains arrive simultaneously. A train of 1996 Tube Stock tailed by 96089 departs to Wembley Park from the northbound platform that was built new for the Jubilee Line in 1979, given this colourful panel work treatment to fit in line with the new stations at Bond Street and Green Park which have a similar colour scheme. (Friday 18 November 2016)

Swiss Cottage was a completely new station when it was opened on the Bakerloo Line extension in 1939, the Metropolitan Line having a station nearby also called Swiss Cottage which closed on 17 August 1940. The station was built with no building at street level, passengers descending stairs down to a sub-surface ticket hall built beneath the big road junction that sits above. The station decoration is uniform with the earlier Underground 1930s extensions, using the standard in-house tiling and colour scheme as well as having the station name frieze incorporated into the tiling along the length of the platform. A 1996 Tube Stock motors out with 96095 on the rear. (Friday 18 November 2016)

Opened on 2 August 1880 by the Metropolitan Railway, Neasden is the location of both the Metropolitan and Jubilee lines' depot, which has been shared since 1979 (1939-1979 as the Bakerloo), and is situated on a site between here and Wembley Park stations in full view of the running lines. This station was the site of a derailment of a train of 1983 Tube Stock and 1986 prototype Tube Stock, of which the best design was to become today's Central Line 1992 Tube Stock. The original Metropolitan Railway station building has been retained at street level and gives a slight idea that when opened, the area around it was still countryside as it is a single storey small country-looking building. A train leaves on a journey to Stratford with 96030 tailing. (Friday 2 December 2016)

Between Kilburn and Neasden, the line is on a downhill gradient and gives trains a bit of extra speed. 1996 Tube Stock 96120 comes to a stop at the island platform at Dollis Hill with its 1930s art deco platform building and canopy. This station was opened on 1 October 1909 by the Metropolitan Railway, before being taken over by the Bakerloo Line in 1939. The Metropolitan Line runs fast through this station, also running parallel to the Chiltern Railways' line into Marylebone, seen on the far right, operated by Diesel Multiple Unit trains. (Friday 2 December 2016)

After a climb, trains reach Willesden Green where its Metropolitan Railway station building, designed by C.W. Clark, has been retained. Clark was the railway's architect at the time, responsible for replacing the original brick structure in 1925. The station has outer platforms on which, very occasionally, Metropolitan Line trains have stopped during Jubilee Line engineering works, but usually hurrying through non-stop is the norm. There are a number of turn-back sidings on this line, as seen here between the two passing trains on this end of the line, the other two being at West Hampstead and Wembley Park stations, helping to allow more trains to serve the Central area and also helping to operate the line in serious disruption. 1996 Tube Stock 96091 rattles over the points into the station as 96085 does likewise on the tail of the departing train towards Stanmore. (Friday 2 December 2016)

The station at Kilburn is situated on the very long Edgware Road and is in walking distance, around 200 metres, of nearby Brondesbury Park station on the North London Line, now part of London Overground. Carrying both the southbound Metropolitan and Jubilee Line tracks, an old Metropolitan Railway bridge is in situ with the company's name and insignia very much in evidence. This stretch of line to Finchley Road is very panoramic, being situated on a viaduct above the rooftops of the suburban houses. A short bus ride takes you to Kilburn High Road and Kilburn Park stations further along Kilburn High Road. 1996 Tube Stock 96032 runs into the station neck and neck with a Chiltern Railways Diesel Multiple Unit seen hiding behind the trackside greenery. (Friday 2 December 2016)

The Central London Railway first opened its station at Bond Street on 24 September 1900 on the section between Shepherd's Bush and Bank; at one time Harry Gordon Selfridge, the owner of the big American style department store on Oxford Street, wanted the station renamed as 'Selfridges', after his store. The station was reconstructed in the early 1970s as part of the new Jubilee Line extension to Charing Cross, with its two intermediate stations being built at Bond Street and Green Park. It retains its colourful 1970s decor that the platforms and some passageways at Baker Street, Bond Street, Green Park, and Charing Cross received when the extension was constructed. The station is seeing further development and reconstruction with the coming of the new Crossrail line between Shenfield and Maidenhead and, like Tottenham Court Road, will make an already busy West End station even busier. (Tuesday 3 January 2017)

London Underground took great advantage of trying out new designs with the building of the new Jubilee Line extension to Stratford, including the use of platform edge doors (PEDs), as seen here, which help prevent people or their possessions falling onto the track and suicide attempts. The new section opened in stages with Phase 1 on Friday 14 May 1999 between Stratford and North Greenwich, phase 2 on 17 September 1999 between North Greenwich and Bermondsey, then to Waterloo on 24 September. London Bridge opened on 7 October with Southwark the following month. Full line running over the entire extension between Green Park and Stratford was achieved on Saturday 20 November 1999, providing good connections to the East, South East, Central, and North West areas of London with trains passing beneath the River Thames four times during their journey. Many of the new stations are built to big, spacious, and airy dimensions as seen here at Canary Wharf. (Sunday 22 January 2017)

West Ham has become a very important interchange for people wanting to access different areas of London; gone are the days of only being served by the District and Hammersmith & City lines and the North London Line which was not the most frequent and reliable suburban line on the section up to North Woolwich. Since the Jubilee Line first started running here on Friday 14 May 1999, the transport links have grown and grown, including the reintroduction of a Platform for the Shoeburyness and Grays trains to serve here. Seen from the Docklands Light Railway platforms – once the North London Line's platforms – we get a good view of the architecture that is almost a modern version of Charles Holden, with streamlined brick structures and use of glass. A 1996 Tube Stock train lead by 96098 enters the station, only travelling as far as Waterloo due to engineering works. (Sunday 22 January 2017)

Chapter 11

Victoria Line

With the introduction of the 2009 Tube Stock on the Victoria Line to replace the original 1967 Tube Stock depicted here, various upgrade work with the signalling system caused the 1967 Tube Stock to only be able to operate on the section of line between Seven Sisters and Brixton towards the end of its working life. On the final day before this section of line between Walthamstow Central and Seven Sisters was switched over to the new signalling, we see unit 3062 waiting to depart from Walthamstow Central. This station was opened with the first stage on 1 September 1968 between Walthamstow Central and Highbury & Islington. (Friday 27 May 2011)

The platform tile motif at Walthamstow Central was designed by Julia Black and is a reproduction of a design by famous textile designer, poet, novelist, translator, and socialist activist William Morris (1834-1896) who was born and lived in Walthamstow. His house was turned into a museum and can be visited today; his works are on display in nearby Lloyd Park. (Sunday 22 January 2017)

The coming of the Victoria Line saw a lot of alteration of platforms, and diverting of lines into newly constructed and aligned tunnels to serve new platforms or to allow cross platform interchange to be provided with the new line. At Finsbury Park, in what is now the southbound Victoria and westbound Piccadilly Line platforms where cross platform interchange is provided, such work was done where the original terminating platforms of the Northern City Line were used. The building of the line was costing a lot of money, so, due to the need to economise on the capital expenditure, it was decided to cut back the Northern City Line a stop before Finsbury Park at Drayton Park. This enabled the two terminal platforms to be used, with a large amount of work having to be done to divert the westbound Piccadilly Line and use of the original Piccadilly Line platforms to accommodate the northbound Victoria and eastbound Piccadilly lines respectively. It is easy to identify the original Northern City Line platforms, because the platform tunnels are built to a bigger dimension than a normal tube line, as the line was originally opened by the Great Northern & City Railway later taken over by the Metropolitan in 1913, with both companies using Mainline gauge trains. A train of 2009 Tube Stock climbs up out of Finsbury Park south to Brixton, all four platforms here are built on a 'hump'. (Sunday 15 January 2017)

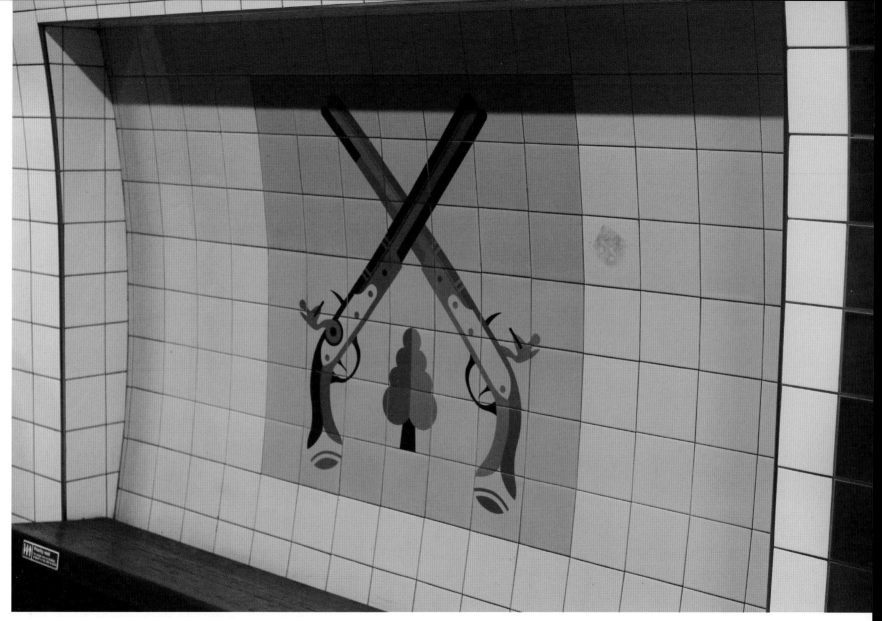

The tile motif here, designed by Tom Eckersley, of two pistols crossed over, depicts the duelling that used to take place here, when Finsbury Park used to be situated on the outskirts of London. Today it is probably hard to imagine that London was much smaller than what we know today! (Sunday 15 January 2017)

King's Cross is one of the line's major interchanges where it connects with the Metropolitan, Hammersmith & City, Circle, Piccadilly, and Northern lines. Interchange is also provided with Mainline trains at King's Cross and St Pancras, as well as international trains at the St Pancras International Eurostar terminal. This station was site to one of the Underground's tragic events when, on the evening of 18 November 1987 at around 19:30, a fire broke out on the Piccadilly Line escalators, caused by a passenger dropping a cigarette that was not extinguished properly down beneath the wooden escalator, causing years of accumulated grease, dirt, and dust to ignite. Sadly, thirty-one people were killed and 100 injured as the fire raged, sending smoke and toxic fumes into the ticket hall and around the platforms. Here is a view along the northbound platform, where the running lines run right to left instead of the usual left to right. This is to aid cross platform interchange with the Northern Line at Euston and the former Northern City Line at Highbury & Islington which is now part of the Hertford loop and Welwyn Garden City line operated by Great Northern.

The tile motif was designed by Tom Eckersley and the picture depicts the name of the station, with five king's crowns all placed in the shape of a cross.

Oxford Circus offers cross platform interchange with the Bakerloo Line, both of which offload many shoppers to the nearby busy Oxford Street and Regent Streets, as well as the famous Carnaby Street. The Central Line also interchanges with both lines here and all three lines are very busy, with this station having had some work done in recent decades to cope with the extra traffic. On 22 November 1984, a fire broke out, starting in the passageway on the northbound Victoria Line platform, causing services to be suspended due to white asbestos being present; thankfully there were no casualties. Services were resumed on the 18 December. The three lines here are also some of the hottest lines all year round; with the trains and many passengers generating lots of heat, London Underground have been trialling many ways to cool stations down effectively and above the train in the platform roof can be seen such a method in the form of fans blowing out cooler air. (Tuesday 10 January 2017)

This Oxford Circus tile motif was designed by Hans Unger and depicts a circle which represents the Circus, with circles forming a cross using the three lines colours that interchange here. The blue dots are in the majority here in that this one is found on the Victoria Line platforms. (Tuesday 10 January 2017)

The line connects with most of the other Underground lines and cuts many journey times; otherwise, passengers would have to go the longer way round with many changes. Also, the line stops for many tourist attractions along its fourteen-mile stretch, aside from Oxford Street. Its most famous stop has to be across nearby Green Park, where Buckingham Palace sits. On 7 March 1969, Her Majesty Queen Elizabeth II opened the section of line between Warren Street and Victoria which was stage 3 of the phased opening. After travelling in the driver's cab and as a passenger in the saloon, (being the only monarch to have travelled on the tube during their reign) she then held a small opening ceremony at her local station, so to speak, Green Park. Another such cooling system can be seen at roof level. (Sunday 27 November 2016)

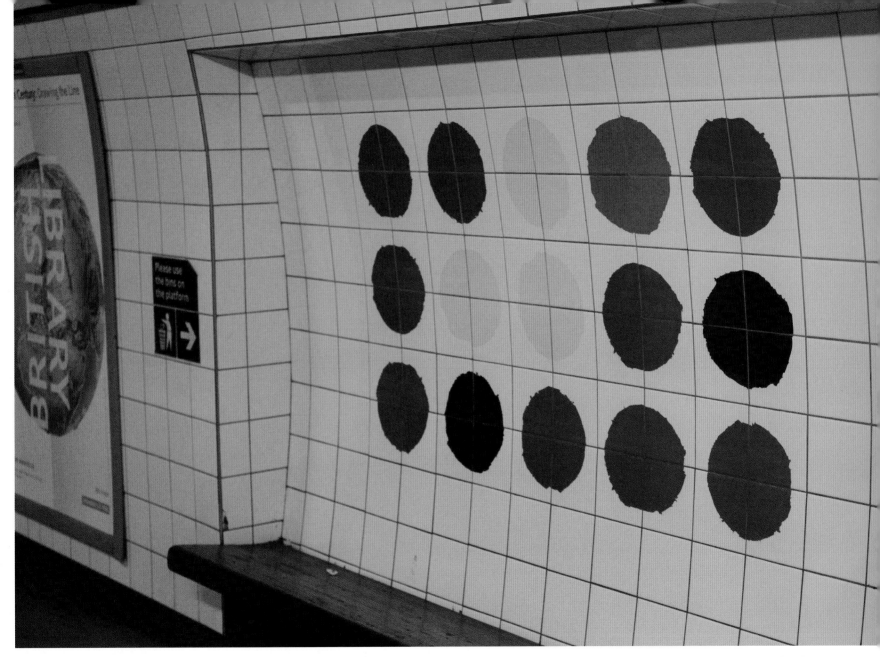

Designed by Hans Unger, the tile motif represents a bird's eye view of the trees in nearby Green Park. (Sunday 27 November 2016)

From the 7 March 1969, Victoria was the line's southern terminus until its final extension south to Brixton on 23 July 1971. To the south of the station, as the train departs, it passes over points that lead to two reversing sidings positioned in between the two running tunnels. Many of the stations on the Underground are receiving upgrade work which has yet to be completed as seen here in this view, with some temporary signs further along and what seems to be a new tile mosaic that was not originally there when the line opened. Above can be seen exposed the original cast iron tunnel segments while work to the roof takes place. (Sunday 27 November 2016)

The motif designed by Edward Bawden at Victoria is of a silhouette of one of the most famous of British monarchs, Queen Victoria, who, prior to our current queen, was our longest reigning monarch (between 20 June 1837 and 22 January 1901). Her home at Buckingham Palace is also a short distance from the area of Victoria and close by to the station; a plaque is displayed in the ticket hall to record the visit by Queen Elizabeth II to open the line in March 1969. (Sunday 27 November 2016)

Pimlico opened the following year after the Brixton extension, opening on 14 September 1972; it is unique in being the only station on the whole line to be exclusively served by the Victoria Line, the rest of the line interchanging with other lines and Mainline railways. Today it serves the famous Tate Britain landmark located nearby. This station has a subsurface ticket hall accessed by means of staircases from street level and until recently retained much of its original wall tiling and station signage, though some has since been replaced. A distinct new feature of the line's platforms was its recessed seating within the wall with its motifs and its design of station name signs with an illuminated background as seen here. (Sunday 27 November 2016)

Pimlico's tile motif does not play on the station's name as with the rest of the lines stations, instead depicting an example of artwork from the nearby Tate Britain gallery. (Sunday 27 November 2016)

Stockwell is the penultimate station of the line before it terminates at Brixton and has cross platform interchange with the Northern Line. This was also the terminus of the City & South London Railway which was the first Underground deep level tube railway in the world, operated by electric trains from the start on 18 December 1890. Upon the Victoria Line's extension through here, the original street level City & South London Railway building was replaced with a more modern building, the third occasion that the station building had been rebuilt to a more modern design. The nearby bus garage of the same name is located around the corner. Here, a train of the 2009 Tube Stock is just pulling into the platform. (Sunday 27 November 2016)

The platform tile motifs were designed as a way of passengers identifying the station they were at and – like Pimlico – it is not overtly obvious but at a guess the zigzags could be a representation of the different roads that converge here. (Sunday 27 November 2016)

Brixton received a new façade at the street level, with upgrade work carried out within the station and has the largest Underground Roundel used anywhere on the system in a big glass display. The works were completed in 2010. The station also received some new tiling, replacing the blue/grey ones from the opening of the original extension. However, at platform level the platform wall has been given new tiling and the tunnel running wall has retained the old tiles allowing passengers to see the before and after. Both platforms have a running tunnel that extends beyond the terminus and is often used to stable trains, as the line's main and only depot is to the north at Northumberland Park, Tottenham. (Sunday 27 November 2016)

Brixton's tile motif plays on its name with a pile of bricks stacked on top of one another. The name Brixton is thought to originate from Brixstane, meaning the stone of Brixi, who was a Saxon lord who erected a boundary stone to mark the meeting place of the ancient Hundred court of Surrey. The former area of the Hundred courts today corresponds to the London Boroughs of Southwark, Lambeth, Wandsworth, Merton, and Richmond upon Thames which were once part of North Surrey. (Sunday 27 November 2016)

Chapter 12

Architecture & Structures

Arnos Grove was opened on 19 September 1932 on the Piccadilly Line's eastbound extension towards Cockfosters. The station building is built in the then popular art deco style designed by in house architect Charles Holden and it has often been described as a significant piece of work of modern architecture. The station received a refurbishment in 2005; however, most of its heritage features were retained due to it being given Grade II listed status in 1971, being upgraded to Grade I* listed status in July 2011. (Wednesday 6 January 2010)

Holland Park's station building is built in the unique uniform style employed by the Central London Railway when it built its early stations; the line was opened between Bank and Shepherd's Bush on the 30 July 1900. Most of the other stations on the original section have either had their station rebuilt over the decades or lost older buildings completely. (Friday 1 January 2016)

Temple was built as part of the Thames Embankment project and the original small District Railway building was replaced by this building around 1911; it is designed by Harry Ford in a neo-Georgian Renaissance style. The station originally had a second entrance on the Embankment facade but this was taken out of use in 1984 and filled in, with the one entrance seen here satisfactory enough for the amount of passenger traffic passing through here today. (Sunday 26 July 2016)

The original 1879 building at Ealing Common was demolished in connection with the Piccadilly Line extension when it was extended from Hammersmith to South Harrow, over the former District tracks on 4 July 1932. The new building was constructed during 1930 and 1931, jointly designed by Charles Holden and Stanley Heaps in a similar style to the 1926 Morden extensions stations which were constructed using Portland stone. This station has Grade II listed status and is served by the District Line to Ealing Broadway and Piccadilly Line to Uxbridge. (Wednesday 3 August 2016)

Sudbury Town station is a Grade I* listed station, and has to be the more impressive out of the two Sudbury Stations on the Piccadilly Line, the other being at Sudbury Hill which is Grade II listed. The original District Railway building was demolished in 1930 and 1931 and replaced by this impressive rectangular square concrete building, which, like most of Holden's station designs, is almost comparable to a mini cathedral rather than a train station. The station retains much of its original station signage that uses the Johnston Delf Smith typeface, which is a wedge-serif variation to the standard Johnston typeface that is used on the London Underground networks signage, publicity, maps etc. Buses still serve stops and terminate on the station forecourt just as they did from the 1930s. (Thursday 29 September 2016)

Situated in Cassiobury Park one mile from Watford Town Centre, Watford station, designed by Metropolitan Railway architect C.W. Clark, was opened on the new Watford branch on 2 November 1925. The Stanmore branch, which opened some years later in 1932, would closely copy the style used on the Watford branch. The station retains a rural outer suburbs feel to it and it was built in a style similar to the houses by which the station is surrounded in Metroland territory. The proposed diversion of the line close to the Grand Union Canal along the disused Croxley Green branch to Watford Junction will see this station abandoned. However, it has Grade II listed status so it should still be standing for many more decades to come. (Friday 9 December 2016)

Originally sited further south on the current site of the Mainline Thameslink tracks, Farringdon was opened as Farringdon Street and was re-located to its current site on 23 December 1865, retaining the original name. The station was renamed to Farringdon & High Holborn, as can be seen in the tile work retained on C.W. Clark's building. Farringdon station was a busy passenger and goods station, seeing freight, cattle, parcels and passengers although the freight and cattle had their own loading/unloading area on a spur off the running lines travelling towards Kings Cross, which has long been bricked up but still remains. The Grade II listed station was renamed on 21 April 1936 and will be an interchange station for the new Crossrail line between Maidenhead and Shenfield when the line is completed in 2018. (Friday 30 December 2016)

South Kensington was originally opened with a standard Fowler-designed building by the Metropolitan Railway but was demolished in 1907 and replaced by white terracotta entrances at each end of the small shopping arcade seen here, designed by George Sherrin. Both entrances display the wrought ironwork seen here displaying the station name and the Metropolitan & District Railways identity; the Metropolitan Railways service through here is now known as the Circle Line. Just to the right can be glimpsed some blood red terracotta tiles on the original Great Northern, Piccadilly & Brompton Railway building designed by Leslie Green. This station building was later taken out of use and today's Piccadilly Line shares the same entrances and ticket hall with the District & Circle lines, access being via escalators and stairs instead of the original lifts. The station and the subways that link the station and the museums are both Grade II listed. (Sunday 1 January 2017)

The Jubilee Line extension through South-East London and Docklands across to Stratford brought a futuristic generation of station design and building architecture and the example at Canary Wharf seen here was opened on the 17 September 1999 by the then Mayor, Ken Livingston. All the stations along the new section have large, airy stations with concrete and metal being the majority of materials used on the buildings and platforms. The buildings use of lots of glass in the design by architect Sir Norman Foster which allows loads of daylight to shine through down the escalator banks to the platform area; this was and is the showpiece station for the extension. (Tuesday 3 January 2017)

Opened as a terminus temporarily for the Bakerloo Line on 31 January 1915, the line arrived at Kilburn Park on the extension from Paddington and was further extended a further stop to the surface at Queen's Park on 11 February 1915. Like most of the Yerkes tube lines, the building is built to the uniform Leslie Green style, and was one of the first of London Underground stations built specifically to use escalators rather than the more common lifts to get passengers to and from platform level. This station is a Grade II listed station. (Wednesday 4 January 2017)

The District and Hammersmith & City Line trains leave the tunnel at Bow Road before climbing a 1 in 28 gradient to the surface, the steepest gradient on the entire network. This Grade II listed station was reputedly designed by C.A. Brereton, an engineer for the Whitechapel & Bow Railway which was later incorporated into the District Line. Although not opened by the District Railway, its station building was built to a design that looks similar to London, Tilbury, & Southend Railway architecture. (Wednesday 4 January 2017)

The 1926 Morden extension brought some very decadent and elegant designs and architecture to the Underground system, reflecting the era of the roaring twenties when Britain and most notably London was starting to recover from the effects of the First World War. This extension would be where we would see some of architect Charles Holden's earliest works of art in partnership with Stanley Heaps. This example at Clapham Common, opened on 3 June 1900, incorporates both the early art deco design which will become more popular in the 1930s and 1940s and the City & South London Railway style, with the rather Victorian-looking roof dome that the station received when it was rebuilt between 29 November 1923 and 30 November 1924, when the Northern Line tunnels and stations were reconstructed to the standard gauge size of the other tube lines then around. To the back of the photographer sits the white painted street entrance to Clapham Common deep level shelter built and used during the Second World War to shelter from the air raids. This station is Grade II listed. (Sunday 8 January 2017)

The system inherited some very antiquated buildings when some of the suburban lines were transferred over to London Underground trains as part of the new works programme. Here, on the Woodford to Hainault branch, we are at Chigwell with its magnificent Great Eastern Railway country style station, which was opened on 1 May 1903. The Central Line stations between Leyton and Epping, and Newbury Park and Woodford retain almost all of their original station buildings with the exception of one or two such as Loughton but most fit in with their countrified surroundings that they retain today, with Chigwell not looking out of place here among the middle class suburban style houses. (Friday 13 January 2017)

Tooting Broadway opened its gates to South Londoners on 13 September 1926 on the extension south to Morden. This station building was designed by Charles Holden and was one of his earliest masterpieces for London Underground, after he was selected by the General Manager of the Underground Electric Railways Company of London (UERL) Frank Pick, who, it is said, grew dissatisfied with the designs that the UERL's in-house architect, Stanley Heaps, was producing. Just like at Wood Green on the Piccadilly Line, this is also a Grade II listed building, sited on the corner of two main roads crossing at a junction sitting comfortably between two different parades of shops. On a cold, wet, dismal day the floodlighting which was used on the exterior of most of Charles Holden station buildings to give a good effect, as well as the interior lights shining through the three large panes of glass complete with Underground roundel gives the intending travellers a sense of warmth and cosiness on days such as this. (Sunday 15 January 2017)

The new Tottenham Court Road station building now takes up a new site on the corner of Charing Cross Road and Oxford Street, replacing the original Central London Railway facade dating from 1900. It has been built to a very modern design with much use of metal materials and will mirror much of the other stations on the new Crossrail route. This station will most certainly see a bigger increase in passenger usage when the new line opens with its two new entrance/exits near Centrepoint, as well as the reconstructed subway outside the Dominion Theatre also helping to cope with this increase. (Sunday 22 January 2017)

This example of a London Transport in-house tile pattern is of the London Transport Griffin which was adopted by London Transport as a crest, appearing on most of the internal documents, uniforms, and even boxes of food and tea bags in the staff canteens, which London Transport made itself for many years. (Wednesday 30 November 2016)

This embossed tile is of the famous St Paul's Cathedral which the Central Line serves at its St Paul's station in the City. (Wednesday 30 November 2016)

This may just look like a ventilation grille from a distance, but when you get a closer look you can see that to make the grille look more pleasing and not disturb the clean design of the platform area at Manor House station, it has been given some decorative artwork. Frank Pick and Lord Ashfield often liked the Underground not only to be fit for purpose, but to also be a nice environment for the passengers to travel in and for what they see to be nice to the eye. This decorative grille, if kept in a clean state would most definitely be nicer to look at than a plain one with large amounts of dust accumulated on it. (Saturday 24 December 2016)

Chapter 13

Signage & Design

For the Underground 150th celebrations in January 2013, a special train was run by the LT Museum and London Underground using a former London Transport steam locomotive, Metropolitan Electric locomotive no.12 *Sarah Siddons* and some former Ashbury coaches between Edgware Road and Moorgate. The terminating bay platforms here at Moorgate received reproductions of these original station name roundels in conjunction with the event and are to the style of roundel that the Metropolitan Railway adopted instead of the bar and circle version of the Underground group of lines, as the Metropolitan Railway was always seen as a superior railway of Mainline status. It would later be standardised like the rest of the lines on the system when it was incorporated into the same ownership in 1933, when the newly formed London Passenger Transport Board (LPTB) was formed. (Friday 8 November 2013)

This film roll theme at Leicester Square station reflects the many cinemas that are situated in the area around the station; both Piccadilly and Northern Line platforms and corridors have this, with this example being from the Piccadilly Line platform. (Tuesday 17 November 2015)

This preserved but still in use sign at Covent Garden station is an example of the original early roundel introduced to the system in 1908. The roundel has evolved many times over the decades since then, but still does the job that it was intended to do very well and is recognised worldwide. There are two further examples still in situ on the system at Caledonian Road and Ealing Broadway. (Tuesday 17 November 2015)

After the Victoria Line was completed and fully operational, the newest extension for the Underground was to Heathrow Airport, which saw new materials and a modern design in architecture, some of which came from the new Victoria Line. At Hatton Cross, the illuminated station name signs used were familiar to passengers who used the Victoria Line. Most of the Victoria Line examples were later replaced by normal signs; however, Pimlico retains its examples. (Sunday 23 October 2016)

The Morden extension was to be the beginning of the Underground's flirtations with new styles in design and architecture. When the London Passenger Transport Board was formed in 1933, and even before that period, the Underground's chief executive and vice chairman, Frank Pick, and chairman, Lord Ashfield, had keen eyes for making sure that everything to do with the group was uniform, nicely designed and fit for purpose. This example of signage displays all of those aims. (Tuesday 22 November 2016)

Bethnal Green with a varied range of signage; note the in-house London Transport tile towards the top of the station name sign and the continuous name frieze also incorporating the stations name in the tile work. (Wednesday 30 November 2016)

Camden Town Night Tube roundel. The lines that operate a Night Tube service at the weekend received one or two roundels like this at certain stations to promote the Night Tube service, in the form of vinyl stickers stuck over the original sign. (Sunday 11 December 2016)

Station name roundel design incorporated into the seating at Canary Wharf Jubilee Line station on the Stratford extension.
(Wednesday 3 January 2017)

Another of the system's historic signs at West Brompton. Note the style of the W in the layout using two letter 'V' overlapping each-other into a 'W'; this style was not adopted into the Johnston typeface font. (Friday 6 January 2017)

'Way Out' sign at Holland Park. (Friday 1 January 2016)

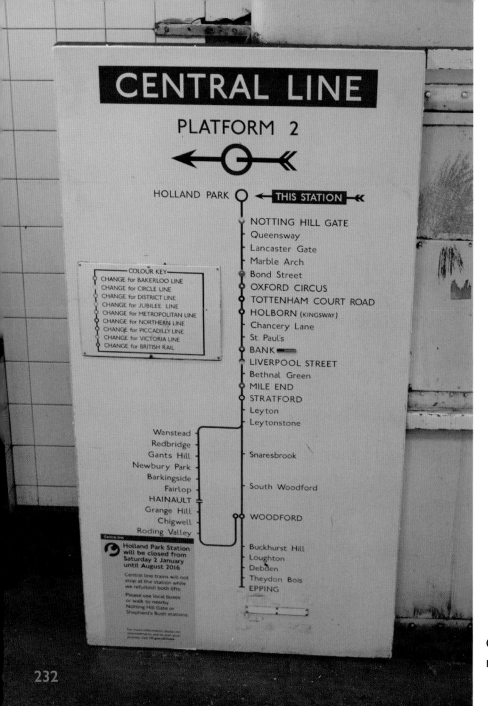

Central line route sign at Holland Park; this has since been replaced by a modern version. (Friday 1 January 2016)

'To The Trains'. This old hand painted sign can still be found on the wall at Stepney Green as you descend the stairs to platform level. (Monday 29 August 2011)

'Underground To The Trains'. This old beautiful sign can be found at Clapham Common station, where you descend to a very old-looking narrow island platform. (Sunday 8 January 2017)

This obscure little sign indicating which platform we are on can be found at Putney Bridge on what used to be the bay platform, but is now the through platform to Wimbledon. (Sunday 26 June 2016)

Aldgate East District and Hammersmith & City Line station. (Friday 30 December 2016)

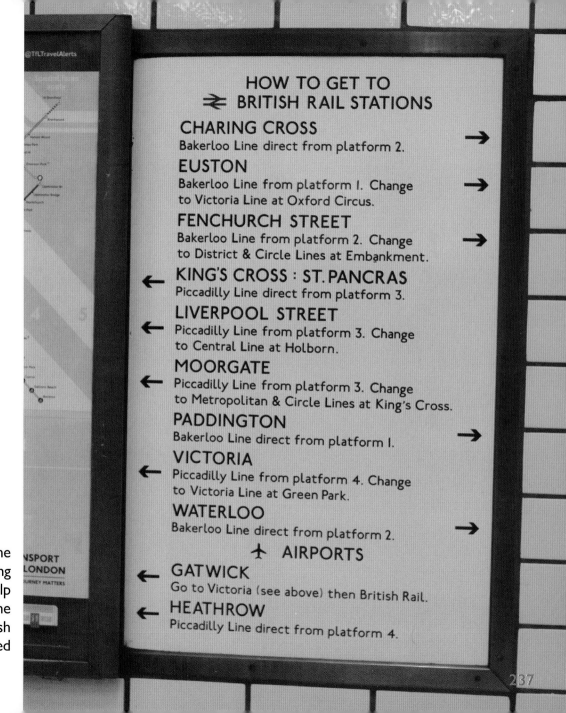

HOW TO GET TO
≋ BRITISH RAIL STATIONS

CHARING CROSS →
Bakerloo Line direct from platform 2.

EUSTON →
Bakerloo Line from platform 1. Change
to Victoria Line at Oxford Circus.

FENCHURCH STREET →
Bakerloo Line from platform 2. Change
to District & Circle Lines at Embankment.

← **KING'S CROSS : ST. PANCRAS**
Piccadilly Line direct from platform 3.

← **LIVERPOOL STREET**
Piccadilly Line from platform 3. Change
to Central Line at Holborn.

← **MOORGATE**
Piccadilly Line from platform 3. Change
to Metropolitan & Circle Lines at King's Cross.

PADDINGTON →
Bakerloo Line direct from platform 1.

← **VICTORIA**
Piccadilly Line from platform 4. Change
to Victoria Line at Green Park.

WATERLOO →
Bakerloo Line direct from platform 2.

✈ AIRPORTS

← **GATWICK**
Go to Victoria (see above) then British Rail.

← **HEATHROW**
Piccadilly Line direct from platform 4.

At Piccadilly Circus, at various locations on the Bakerloo and Piccadilly Line platforms and landing area at the bottom of the escalator, these signs help would-be travellers find their quickest route to the various Mainline termini. Note the name British Rail that is used this organisation now privatised as National Rail. (Sunday 15 January 2017)

PICCADILLY LINE

PLATFORM 3 →
SOUTHBOUND

HOLBORN
LEICESTER SQUARE
PICCADILLY CIRCUS
EARL'S COURT

A sign provided next to the Victoria Line platform at Finsbury Park where cross platform interchange is provided with the Piccadilly Line. (Sunday 15 January 2017)

When the early tube lines were built, the various railway companies never provided the many station name signs dotted along the platform like we see today in the form of the roundel. The early rolling stock had numerous gatemen on the train that opened and closed the gate for passengers to board and alight and the gatemen in the first and last cars usually shouted out the station names, which is why the station name was incorporated into the tiling at the front and back end of the train, as here at Camden Town. There are only a small number of stations retaining this on the Bakerloo, Piccadilly, and Northern lines. (Sunday 11 December 2016)

Edgware Road, Bakerloo line. (Saturday 24 December 2016)

Gillespie Road, (Renamed Arsenal). (Saturday 21 January 2017)

Egyptian Mummy mural at Holborn. (Tuesday 31 January 2017)

Chapter 14

Depots & Installations

Depots

Aside from Acton Works and the train building factory at Bombardier, many of the individual lines' depots carry out light and sometimes heavy maintenance work such as wheel lathing, replacement of wheel sets and motors etc. The depots also provide space for stabling trains at the end of service where they are cleaned and prepared to take up service the following day. The depot is an off limit part of the network, but rare depot open days sometimes allow an inside look to what happens behind the scenes.

Installations

The system has many installations some of which are not always visible or accessible to the general public. In this chapter we take a look at some of these.

Over the 2009 August Bank Holiday weekend, London Underground held an open day at Upminster depot, giving locals and enthusiasts a view into areas that would not usually have been permitted to the public, with the proceeds from the admission fee donated to charity. The depot had a similar open day in 1993, when a steam train operated a shuttle service between Upney and the depot. D stocks 7075 and 7047 are seen stabled in the sidings at the side of the main depot building and were two of the many trains stabled this day due to engineering works between Upminster and a point further west. (Sunday 30 August 2009)

The Underground operates many types of signals that help keep the drivers and the many passengers that they are carrying in their trains safe. Many of the main signals have a trainstop device, known as a tripcock which prevents a train passing it when it is displaying a red aspect, as shown here at Hainault on the Central Line. With the coming of Automatic Train Operation on certain lines, such signals have now disappeared, depending on the type of system that was installed. (Friday 18 November 2016)

The system has range of differing styles of destination indicator boards. Some are very old and still in use, working alongside more modern examples of dot matrix indicators, which have advanced a lot since first trialled at St James's Park station in 1983. This example is seen at Earl's Court still in everyday use, with modern dot matrix indicators provided here too. (Saturday 21 January 2017)

The first escalator installed on the Underground system was at Earl's Court station in 1911 and the early design has evolved into the style we see today, which went on to replace many of the early lifts at many stations where such conversion work could be carried out practically. This example dates from 1939 at St John's Wood, when the Bakerloo Line was extended on the Stanmore branch. Many of the 1930s extensions to Underground lines had a similar style to this with the uplighters provided up the escalators. After the King's Cross fire, all the escalators started to be replaced with fire resistant materials; however, Greenford being an open air station retained its wooden escalator treads until they were replaced by a new design of lift. (Friday 18 November 2016)

Many stations retain the method of lifts getting passengers from street to platform level and their many emergency stairs, which at some stations number over 100 steps. The lifts at Holland Park had its older lifts replaced in 2016, causing the station to close for a number of months to allow the works to be done. Each lift is replaced after a certain number of years of service. (Sunday 22 January 2017)

Uplighter at Southgate. This style of lighting is unique to the Charles Holden-designed stations, specifically on the Piccadilly Lines Cockfosters extension, giving them an atmospheric ambient feeling at these special stations. (Saturday 24 December 2016)

Clock incorporating the roundel in place of the clock face numbers at Bethnal Green. (Wednesday 30 November 2016)

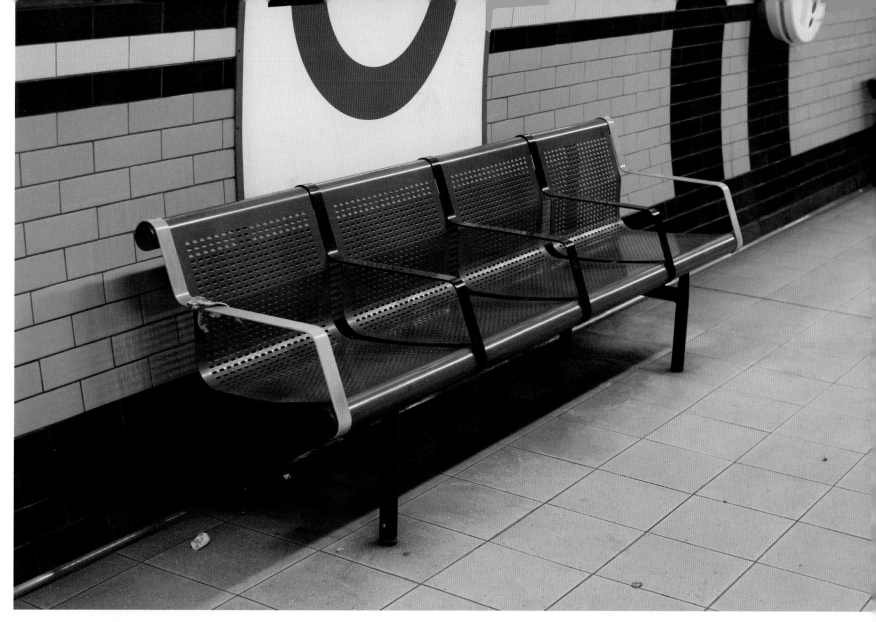

This style of seating is the standard design on most of the network; however, a number of stations have a different style depending on whether it is a heritage listed station, had a refurbishment, or simply retained its old furniture to retain its historic feel. These examples are at Arsenal station on the westbound platform. (Saturday 21 January 2017)

This new digital escalator sign can be found at Piccadilly Circus station where it displays such messages as 'Stand on the right, walk on the left', and even tells passengers that 'You are coming to the end of the escalator'. Whether this will be rolled out network-wide is not known. (Sunday 15 January 2017)

The automatic ticket barriers have evolved greatly since they were first introduced on the newly built Victoria Line at the end of the 1960s. The example here at Holland Park is the latest design of barrier, and is a great improvement compared to the ones from the 1980s and 1990s. (Sunday 22 January 2017)

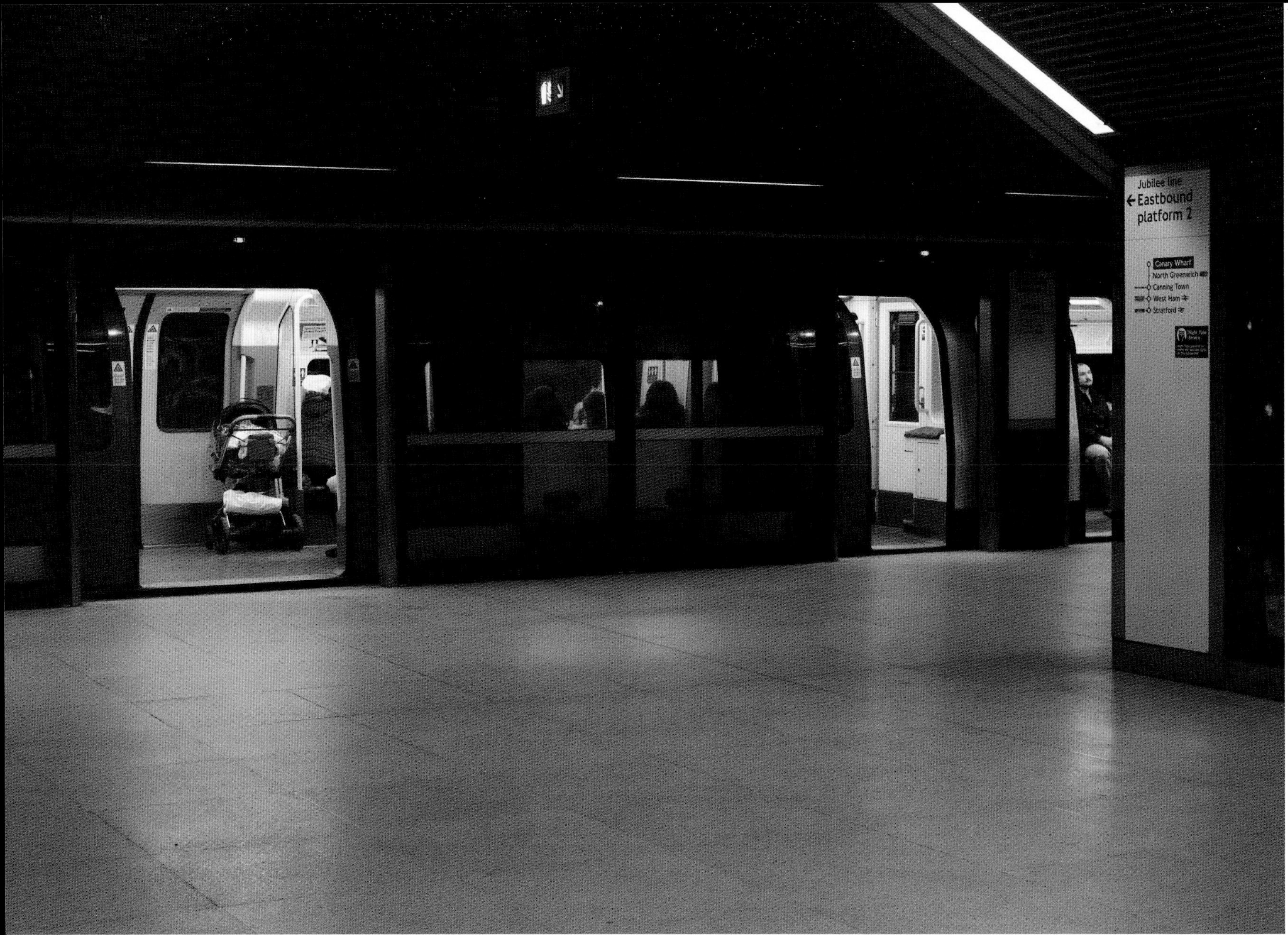
Jubilee line
← Eastbound
platform 2
Canary Wharf
North Greenwich
Canning Town
West Ham
Stratford

The new Jubilee Line extension saw the introduction of new platform edge doors, which open and close in synchronisation with the train doors when it is stationary in the platform, at stations between Westminster and North Greenwich. (Sunday 22 January 2017)

Chapter 15

Rolling Stock

D Stock

The D Stock served on the 'Main' District Line (Edgware Road to High Street Kensington section excluded) for thirty-seven years after the first train entered service on Monday 28 January 1980. The D Stock comprised of seventy-five six car trains (with around eight trains left as of the end of January 2017) and replaced the vintage flare sided CO/CP and R Stocks, between 1981 and 1983. These trains were very unique in that they used the same tube sized wheels as the 1973 Tube Stock, allowing the trains to be built with greater headroom in the saloons. This stock was original delivered and entered service with fixed Windows but due to problems with the forced ventilation, hopper windows were later fitted to three of the five saloon Windows. This stock would settle down to become London Undergrounds most reliable fleet on the system. Here, on the final day of D Stock in passenger service we see Motor Car 7007 leading the last train out of West Kensington on one of its journeys to Upminster, with the enthusiastic driving giving a short burst of the whistle on departure. (Friday 21 April 2017).

After refurbishment of the fleet started, the trailer car of the prototype refurbishment unit kept its trial hand rail fittings and panelling, with the only minor noticeable changes being the passenger doors being painted from white to the charcoal grey colour and the moquette and floor covering design changed to the refurbishment design. Also of note is the rails that run alongside the draught screen by the doorway to assist people on and off the train not being adopted in the final refurbishment design. Trailer car 17008 from the unit is seen here at Upminster. (Tuesday 3 August 2010)

The standard design that the fleet received for its refurbishment, seen in this interior view taken at Tower Hill. (Wednesday 4 January 2017)

S Stock

The S Stock is a standardised train fleet designed to replace the A, C, & D sub-surface Stocks which are all built to differing lengths and dimensions, which restrict certain stocks being able to be used on certain sections of the sub-surface network. With the arrival of this new stock, trains are permitted to run on all sections of the sub-surface network unrestricted, although trains are formed into two differing lengths the seven-car version (S7) works the District, Hammersmith & City and Circle lines replacing six-car C and D Stock, with the eight-car version (S8) replacing the eight-car A Stock. These trains have walk-through saloons allowing improved capacity during busy periods, better security for passengers, and providing an increase in space for standing passengers. These trains have air conditioning, the first for any of the Underground's rolling stock, have every axle motored to allow faster acceleration, with the use of regenerative braking to return current back to the tracks saving energy. One downside of this stock is that they are replacing trains with more comfortable seating with a mix of transverse and longitudinal seats, the S Stock being all longitudinal seating with the exception of the S8 variant that has some transverse seats each car. An S8 variant pulls into West Harrow on the Metropolitan Line. (Friday 2 December 2016)

1972 Tube Stock

The 1972 Tube Stock comprised two batches; the Mk I batch ordered for the Northern Line to replace some trains of the classic 1938 Tube Stock which were starting to get worn out after many years of good service and the Mk II batch ordered for the Jubilee Line. These also worked on the Northern Line for a time, until they were transferred to the Bakerloo Line to work before its Stanmore branch was transferred to the Jubilee Line in 1979. These trains were very similar to the 1967 Tube Stock which operated on the Victoria Line from opening until 2011, but all three had minor technical differences; for example, the Mk Is had cab door number plate stencils to display the train number located in the front cab door whereas the Mk II had an electronic number box located in its offside cab window. Some of the Mk I cars were reformed into the 1967 Tube Stock and the Mk II batch, with this stock still trundling up and down the Bakerloo Line today with trains rumoured to be replaced around 2026. A train accelerates out of Harlesden with 3557 at the rear.

1973 Tube Stock

As part of the plans for the new Heathrow Airport extension from Hounslow West in the early 1970s, London Transport decided it was going to order some new rolling stock for the extension which were to a modern design and were specially tailored for travellers with luggage. These trains comprised of 87½ six-car trains and were built to a slightly longer length than the 1959 Tube Stock trains they replaced and also aided in replacing a seven-car train with a longer six-car train. They had bigger stand back areas in the doorway so that passenger luggage could be placed safely out the way of obstructing passenger movement onto or off the train at stations. The first train entered service in July 1975, when the first phase of the extension to Heathrow opened between Hounslow West and Hatton Cross and after many extensions at Heathrow, these hard-working workhorses still rumble up and down the Piccadilly Line to this day. One unit was scrapped prematurely as it was the unit involved in the 7/7 bombing at Russell Square. Here the Night Tube liveried train departs Alperton with 252 at the rear. For the 2017 leaf fall season two double ended units have had special sandite equipment fitted to the trailer cars, and the units used for sandite duties one for the eastern end and one for the western end of the Piccadilly Line. (Thursday 8 December 2016)

1992 Tube Stock

The 1992 Tube Stock originated from the best of three prototype tube trains that entered trial service between May 1988 and August 1989 running up and down the Jubilee Line, when a derailment at Neasden caused by some equipment becoming detached from the train halted the trials and saw the trains withdrawn. Much of the design for the 1992 Tube Stock comes from the Metro-Cammell-designed Green train C; a Motor Car of this train can be seen preserved at the London Transport Museum's Acton Depot. The first train entered service on the 7 April 1993 on the Central Line and began replacing the veteran 1962 Tube Stock and at the same time bringing an gradual end to guards on the line, with the Waterloo & City Line, still owned by British Rail at this time, also ordering a batch to replace its 1940 Southern Railway origin cars with the first train entering passenger service on 19 July 1993. Both line's trains have in recent years received improvement work and refreshes to the interiors and exteriors, with the Waterloo & City Line retaining the plastic arm rests they were delivered with, the Central Line having lost its arm rests earlier on, not long after being put into service. Although these trains were made to a modern design with many safety improvements, they have proven to be troublesome in service with many failures and even derailments occurring due to equipment becoming detached from the car body; perhaps the derailment with the trial train was a warning! Despite the trouble these trains have given, they have now passed the twenty year mark and are still giving service as 91213 brings in a train for Northolt at Snaresbrook station. (Tuesday 21 November 2016)

1995 Tube Stock

The 1995 Tube Stock was ordered as part of the Northern Line modernisation and upgrade plan, replacing the 1959 Tube Stock trains which in many respects were updated versions of the 1938 Tube Stock, at the same time replacing the last remaining London Underground guards. The first train entered service on 12 June 1998 in One Person Operation mode gradually replacing the remaining 1959/62 Tube Stock and 1972 Mk I Tube Stock trains until, on 27 January 2000, the last 1959 Tube Stock and the last ever guard on the Underground operated. Unlike the similar 1996 Tube Stock, these trains were delivered as seven-car trains and in the last few years these trains have received an interior and exterior refresh and now operate in Automatic Train Operation mode after the line had its signalling upgraded. Here, an example with 51552 accelerates out of Chalk Farm on its way to Edgware. (Saturday 24 December 2016)

Here can be seen the pre-refresh interior that these trains were delivered with, the brighter more modern looking post-refresh interior has improved the appearance of this stock greatly. (Friday 19 September 2014)

Post-refresh interior. (Saturday 30 November 2013)

1996 Tube Stock

The 1996 Tube Stock was delivered as six-car trains and is similar in design and appearance to the 1995 Tube Stock; however, both have different motor equipment notable by the sounds that they both make. This stock was ordered as part of the new Jubilee Line Stratford extension with the Charing Cross terminus being abandoned. They replaced the 1983 Tube Stock, which some had only been in service for ten years, after plans to refurbish this stock to operate the new extension would have been found too costly compared to ordering new rolling stock. The first passenger train entered service on 24 December 1997 between Wembley Park and Charing Cross, although various ceremonial and special trips had been run previously. These trains later received a seventh car with the increase in passenger usage the extension brought and today these seven car trains run in Automatic Train Operation mode. Queensbury see two trains as 96091 departs leaving a train for Central London in the platform. (Thursday 13 October 2016)

2009 Tube Stock

The 2009 Tube Stock was ordered to replace the 1967 Tube Stock between July 2009 and June 2011 on the Victoria Line as part of the line and signalling upgrade, which had been operating on the line since opening in 1969. With the Victoria Line's tunnels being built to slightly larger than the standard dimensions, the chance was taken to build these trains to a wider dimension offering more car space for passengers, the only downfall of this is that they are unable to operate on any other lines, making journeys back to places such as Acton Works or the Bombardier factory for example for modifications and other works only possible by road haulage. The trains have 75 per cent of their axle motored, allowing faster acceleration and higher line speeds to be achieved cutting journey times, with a train of 2009 Tube Stock also being three metres longer and having more seats and room for standing passengers than a train of 1967 Tube Stock, giving a 19 per cent increase in capacity. 2009 Tube Stock 11034 represents the fleet as it departs from Seven Sisters at the rear of this southbound train to Brixton. (Tuesday 31 January 2017)

Chapter 16

Engineer's Rolling Stock

The Underground now has a very expanse range of engineering vehicles in its fleet both on and off the rails, some adapted to be used on both. Here at Chiswick Park on one quiet afternoon, we see battery locomotive L45, which has been adapted to operate on the lines which use Automatic Train Operation denoted by the blue painted body sides, although it is still possible for it to operate on the lines where manual operation is still the norm. Many of the battery locomotives are very old but after refurbishments and heavy overhauls they still continue to serve the Underground system faithfully during non-service hours, although they are becoming a more common sight on the system in daylight hours too. (Thursday 21 February 2008)

This example is L30, which has been refurbished and upgraded with slightly bigger cab windows so the driver has a clearer view, as well as new high intensity headlights and hand rails for ease of movement safely for staff. This was one of two at Mansion House propelling the newly restored coach 353 which was used during the Underground 150th celebrations. (Wednesday 17 July 2013)

Rail Adhesion and Track Recording Trains

Two units of A Stock were retained as part of the Rail Adhesion Train which operates each season during the autumn, when a specially-adapted trailer car is inserted into the middle making the unit into five cars. The trailer releases a special sand/gel mix called sandite that covers the running lines, preventing a build-up of the hard, slippery coating that fallen leaves create when they drop on the line, causing trains wheels to slide and difficulties when braking. The A Stock began entering service from June 1961 on the Metropolitan Line replacing the vintage compartment type trains some of which used to be steam-hauled coaches, later converted into electric trains. Two different batches were ordered; the A60 batch was ordered for the Amersham electrification and Watford line, the A62 batch for the Uxbridge service, replacing the F Stock. Theses trains also operated the self-contained East London line from 1977 and apart from a period when they were replaced by D Stock for a couple of years when the A Stock was being converted to OPO, stayed until the line was closed for upgrade work and taken over by the London Overground network. The 2016 season saw the train make visits on the Piccadilly Line between Ealing Common and Rayners Lane and is seen just coming round the bend into Alperton, and could be heard long before it approached here at Alperton with that distinctive A Stock noise. (Thursday 8 December 2016)

At White City we see the Central Lines western end Rail Adhesion Train has just arrived from West Ruislip and takes a few minutes in the centre platform before taking its scheduled path to Ealing Broadway. Unlike its east end counterpart which is formed of 8 cars, the west end unit is only formed of 5 cars. (Friday 10 October 2017)

The 1960 Tube Stock was once a small fleet of experimental prototype motor cars that were built to test designs and equipment for the next generation of trains, to replace the ageing standard stock that dated from the 1920s and were getting very worn out after many years of exceptional service on the Central Line. The trains were originally formed into six four-car formations, using two converted Standard Stock trailers, which were painted white to match the unpainted aluminium finish of the new motor cars and later in the 1970s these were replaced by single trailer cars of 1938 Tube Stock, when some withdrawn trains of this stock made them surplus. The first train entered service in November 1960 and in 1964, their train equipment was converted to test the Automatic Train Operation system that would later be used for the new Victoria Line that was under construction. Many of the train's features were incorporated into the new lines 1967 Tube Stock. These trains worked the Hainault to Woodford branch for many years and would share the branch with some four car units of 1967 Tube Stock until such workings ended in the 1980s. The remaining 1960 Tube Stock ended their days travelling up and down through the Essex countryside between Epping and Ongar, painted into LT Red with cream window surrounds until the branch closed on 30 September 1994. That unit is now preserved by the Cravens Heritage Trains, and another of the unit was converted by London Underground into a Track Recording Train with a 1973 Tube Stock trailer car specially converted for the job. Here, we see the train sitting next to a larger D Stock at Upminster on the District Line, being of tube size and the role it was converted for sees the train visit all the lines except for the Waterloo & City Line. (Thursday 18 October 2012)

The Underground does not just have engineering vehicles that are confined to the rails, they have vehicles that are capable of operating as both rail and road vehicles, as well as just road vehicles for jobs such as collecting rubbish, delivering parts, as well as to attend to emergencies on the system. Here we see two examples of new Emergency Response Unit vehicles, which look similar to a London Fire Brigade engine. The previous Mayor of London, Boris Johnson, had incorporated the British Transport Police under the TfL umbrella and in the process, the Emergency Response Unit was given an emergency service status which means they are able to travel to locations where there is an emergency, just as emergency services would, meaning help can be gained quicker. Here 2594 is parked up on the Museum depot/Ealing Common depot approach road at Acton Town with an unidentified stable mate parked behind it. (Thursday 8 December 2016)